Praise for *Stripped*

"If you have ever wondered why the road you travel with Christ has taken a sudden, unexpected turn, this book will be a companion to you. If have longed for more of Christ yet found yourself stripped of all you thought you knew, this book will be a lighthouse in the darkness. If you have been tempted to quit, read on. You are not alone and the real adventure is just beginning."

—SHEILA WALSh, author and teacher

"*Stripped* will stir you up to live for Jesus Christ with greater resolve and focus than ever. Lina writes from her heart. She is able to communicate God's Word with purposeful clarity and God-given anointing. If you've ever felt called by God but find yourself daunted by the unexpected difficulty of the road, get ready for some answers."

—CHRISTINE CAINE, author of *Undaunted* and cofounder of the A21 Campaign

"In her raw and relevant book *Stripped*, my friend Dr. Lina reveals the often painful yet necessary process God uses to prepare us to be vessels that carry His glory. Read it and be remade!"

—LISA BEVERE, author and speaker

STRIPPED

When God's Call Turns from
"Yes!" to "Why Me?"

Lina AbuJamra

Moody Publishers

CHICAGO

All Scripture quotations, unless otherwise indicated, are taken from *The Holy Bible, English Standard Version.* Copyright © 2000, 2001 by Crossway Bibles, a division of Good News Publishers. Used by permission. All rights reserved.

Scripture quotations marked NIV are taken from the Holy Bible, New International Version®, NIV® Copyright © 1973, 1978, 1984, 2011 by Biblica, Inc.™ Used by permission of Zondervan. All rights reserved worldwide. www.zondervan.com. The "NIV" and "New International Version" are trademarks registered in the United States Patent and Trademark Office by Biblica, Inc.™

Scripture quotations marked NKJV are taken from the *New King James Version.* Copyright © 1982 by Thomas Nelson, Inc. Used by permission. All rights reserved.

Scripture quotations marked KJV are taken from the King James Version.

Edited by Bailey Utecht
Interior design: Ragont Design
Cover design: DogEared Design, LLC
Cover image:: iStockphoto
Author photo: Caroline Wasko

Library of Congress Cataloging-in-Publication Data

AbuJamra, Lina.
  Stripped : when God's call turns from yes! to why me? / Lina AbuJamra.
    pages cm
  Includes bibliographical references.
  ISBN 978-0-8024-0965-2
  1. Submissiveness—Religious aspects—Christianity. 2. Vocation—Christianity.
I. Title.
BV4647.A25A28 2013
248.4--dc23
                                                          2013016132

We hope you enjoy this book from Moody Publishers. Our goal is to provide high-quality, thought-provoking books and products that connect truth to your real needs and challenges. For more information on other books and products written and produced from a biblical perspective, go to www.moodypublishers.com or write to:

Moody Publishers
820 N. LaSalle Boulevard
Chicago, IL 60610

1 3 5 7 9 10 8 6 4 2

Printed in the United States of America

To my brothers and sisters in Christ
who have answered the call to be stripped
without ever looking back.

"I have decided to follow Jesus,
no turning back, no turning back."

CONTENTS

I DIDN'T SEE IT COMING

It is doubtful God can bless a man greatly until He has hurt him deeply. —A. W. TOZER

My story is as cliché as it gets.

It was a perfect Wisconsin summer night. The moon was radiant. The ripple of a distant creek echoed in the silence. The air was warm enough to leave my jacket behind but cool enough to breathe. It was summer camp at its best. Parents felt millions of miles away and decisions could be made without the distractions of lesser things.

I don't remember exactly what the preacher said on that particular night, but I can still smell the rock that I stood on as I gazed upward and felt closer to God than I'd ever felt before. And in that moment I knew that my life was forever changed.

No more living for myself. No more personal agendas and temporary gains. No more questions without answers and independent days. It was like color suddenly burst into my life for the first time, and I was no longer the same.

I should probably explain a few things to you that had led up to that dramatic point in my life. I was by no means new to Christianity. I was born in Beirut, Lebanon, and don't remember a time in my life when I didn't know about Jesus.

One of my earliest childhood memories was the night I accepted Jesus Christ into my heart as my Savior. Looking back, I'm sure I did it mostly out of fear, but who can blame a seven-year-old for wanting to escape the burning heat of hell? The truth is that I really did like this Jesus I had heard so much about in Sunday school, and if He had died to buy my way into heaven, then I was more than willing to sign up.

Some people believe in love at first sight. They claim to tumble head over heels in love with someone at first glance. Others swear that love comes softly, unexpectedly, even quietly. My love for Jesus Christ was a little bit of both.

For years Christ had quietly but persistently beckoned me to Him until I finally tumbled head over heels in love with Him on that warm Wisconsin summer night. I was only sixteen years old but old enough to know that my life would never be the same again. Jesus loved me despite my sin. He was alive, and He lived in me. But more than that, He was crying out my name, declaring me His own. He loved me. He knew everything about me and still chose me. My heart had finally found its home.

That night was a turning point for me. It was the night I gave the reins of my life over to God. I wanted, even longed for God to lead me where He wanted me to go. I was on top of the world with Jesus as my guide and the future in His sight. I not only wanted to live for God, but as I stood on that rock, I wanted to climb steep mountains for Him and proclaim His name from the highest peaks for the whole world to hear.

God had wrecked me forever with His love, and I was ready for the adventure to begin. With God on my side, what could ever go wrong?

Little did I know that the worst was yet to come.

I work in an ER, so my life work is taking care of people

facing crises. By far and above, the most common response people give me when facing a crisis of significant magnitude is this: I didn't see it coming. Ask the parents who've just been told their six-year-old daughter has leukemia, or the fourteen-year-old teenager facing an unplanned pregnancy. Few people predict the unexpected turbulence ahead. Lives that are filled with blissful joy today can suddenly become bumpy and hard, but few people make plans that take into account the impossible road that is sure to come.

A careful consideration of each situation should indicate otherwise. There are always red flags along the way. There is always some writing on the wall predicting the obstacles ahead, but we rarely pay attention to them.

IT IS THE stripping that makes the man or woman fit for Christ.

As I stood on that rock on that warm summer night, little could I have predicted what was to come in my life. I certainly did not anticipate the stripping that would follow. Instead of peaks and mountains, I would become familiar with the pits and the valleys. Instead of victories and successes, I would soon learn how to survive the battle that would rage on every front. As the moon smiled down on my head, little could I have predicted the sin that would continue to plague me, and the scars that would one day distinguish me as a follower of Jesus Christ. But most of all, I could not have predicted the pain of Christ's call. No one plans on a journey through pain, yet pain is often the road that God chooses to purify His children.

I should have seen it coming. After all, the writing was on

the wall, or rather, it's in God's book—the Bible. Starting in the Old Testament and all the way through to Revelation, we are given story after story of God's people who were stripped for His glory. They came to Him with great expectation and hope, ceding their rights to themselves. They expected relief. They expected deliverance. What they missed was that God's road to deliverance usually begins with Him stripping His followers of the things that must go and transforming them into vessels fit to be used for His purposes alone.

Psalm 66:10–12 says it best: "For you, O God, have tested us; you have tried us as silver is tried. You brought us into the net; you laid a crushing burden on our backs; you let men ride over our heads; we went through fire and through water; yet you have brought us out to a place of abundance."

On that warm summer night, I had drawn a line in the sand declaring myself Christ's follower. I had said yes to the One who promised to give me life. I was about to find out that when a person answers the call of the Savior, it is by far the best decision in the world, but also the hardest. After all, answering the call of Jesus of Nazareth means following the example of the One who was stripped for our sakes. Yet it is the stripping that makes the man or woman fit for Christ. It is the stripping that allows greater usefulness for the King. It is the stripping that distinguishes the true saint from the casual observer. And it is the stripping that allows us to finally reach the place of abundance in Christ.

MY NEXT MAJOR BREAKTHROUGH

Now fast-forward with me fifteen years to the year 2002. I was no longer the innocent sixteen-year-old kid at summer camp. My heart was far more deeply in love with Jesus than ever before. I was well-seasoned in pain, having already been stripped of much from my life, but I still longed for more. I had, after all, seen the face of my Savior. I had tasted His presence, and nothing else would ever satisfy me again.

I decided to do a three-day fast for a greater breakthrough in my relationship with the Lord. Every Christian who I greatly admired fasted so I figured I should try it too.

The fast paid off. On a quiet New Year's Day, while the rest of the world watched college football, the Lord Jesus Christ called me to full-time vocational ministry.

I suppose this time I should have expected His call, but I tend to be easily blindsided by the obvious. We're told in Habakkuk 2:1 that the prophet stood at the watchpost, looking out to see what God would say to him—and God answered him. God always welcomes our hunger for a divine encounter with an answer. And much like the prophet Habakkuk, I had been standing on my watchpost begging for God to use me somewhere, somehow, anyhow.

So it shouldn't have come as a surprise to me that God would call me to full-time ministry. I would have done anything for Him. This time, though, I felt as if surely, the worst was behind me. I was no longer a beginner Christian. My life for Him was about to really begin. I would finally reap the richness of a life dedicated to the risen Jesus. I dreamed of the joys of serving Jesus full time. I wondered how God would take a pediatric emergency room doctor and transform her into His full-time servant. I could almost taste the fullness of joy that lay ahead.

Once again, I'd forgotten that God cares less about our

titles and our jobs and more about our heart and our character. Once again, I'd forgotten that the Christian walk is one of a deeper stripping and a deeper equipping leading to the total transformation of the man and woman for Christ.

In other words, once again, I didn't see it coming. It wouldn't take long for my "yes" to become "Why me, Lord? Why did you choose me? Why is this happening to me?"

The next ten years would stretch me and push me to the brink of my faith like never before. At times it felt as if my soul was being defibrillated as God continued to strip even more of the layer after layer of gruff and self and carnality from my life.

At one point I didn't think I'd survive. But deep in my soul was the quiet certitude that I was held by the One who loves me so deeply that He had given His own life for me.

> **IT WOULDN'T** take long for my "yes" to become "Why me, Lord?"

He would never strip anything from my life that He doesn't know must go. In Proverbs 25:4 God says, "Take away the dross from the silver, and the smith has material for a vessel." I had asked to be the kind of vessel that God could use for His purposes. God was committed to making me that kind of vessel too.

This book is my attempt to describe the stripping process that every follower of Jesus Christ must go through in order to become more like Christ and better equipped for His use.

Many times I almost quit. I'll tell you more about it in the next pages. Many times I wondered at my sanity; many times I doubted God's call and His love for me. But not for a moment has the Savior forsaken me. The very hand that stripped me has also been the hand of my loving Father that has held me near to His heart. He has always seen far more in me than I ever could have seen, and has had more in mind for me than I ever could have imagined.

This book is for every person who longs for more but is often surprised that the road to more usually begins with pain—the pain of being stripped.

I can't think of a single time in my life when I didn't feel God stripping me down. Every time I start to feel the slightest bit comfortable, there is another rock thrown into my path, another mountain to climb or get around.

I have been homeless, without a car, and struggling to have food on the table for my kids. I have been lonely, friendless, and in physical pain.

He has stripped me of my own goals, plans, and ideas. He has stripped me of my desires, ambitions, and wants.

I think this process will continue as long as there is anything keeping me from being as close to Him as He wants me to be.

—DARLENE

Part One

ANSWERING THE CALL TO BE STRIPPED

Chapter One

CAN YOU HEAR ME NOW?

Wherever God's finger points, His hand will clear a way.
—L. B. C. COWMAN

Why would anyone answer a call that promises pain with stark certainty? What kind of strategy would use the promise of pain and suffering as its primary recruiting method?

The phone rings. I glance over. I don't recognize the number. Should I pick up and hope it's the call I've been waiting my whole life for, or do I let it go to voice mail?

The most compelling reason to answer any call is directly related to the importance of the one calling. It's no wonder that most telemarketers don't identify themselves on caller ID.

Now go back with me about two thousand years ago to a small seaside town in Galilee. It's a regular day and fishermen are doing their usual thing: fishing. A man by the name of Jesus approaches a cluster of fishermen. Here's how it played out according to Matthew 4:18–20:

> While walking by the Sea of Galilee, he saw two brothers, Simon (who is called Peter) and Andrew his brother, casting a net into the sea, for they were fishermen. And he said to them, "Follow me, and I will make you fishers of men." Immediately they left their nets and followed him.

How could two words—*follow me*—so radically change the lives of two grown men with stable fishing careers and comfortable, secure lives? Jesus' command was simple. Follow me. In return, He made a promise. "I will make you fishers of men."

Did Peter and Andrew initially misunderstand the call? Were they hoping that Jesus would turn their local fishing gig into a worldwide multimillion-dollar operation? Did they dream of a reality fishing show and national fame? It's hard to tell, but one thing is certain. Peter and Andrew were forever changed in that moment.

I often wonder if Peter and Andrew knew what lay ahead for them in the years to come. I wonder what Peter and Andrew would have done had they been warned that this same Jesus would one day die on a cross, and that eventually Peter himself would be killed upside down on the same kind of cross?

I find myself very much like Peter and Andrew. I respond to the call of Jesus with a pretty good idea of what I want Him to do for me. While I dream of worldly comforts and temporary solutions to my earthly problems, Christ's vision for my life far exceeds the one that I have for my own. His main focus is fixed on what He wants to do in me. It is His grace that keeps us from knowing all that lies ahead for us lest we turn and run while we still can.

I RESPOND TO the call of Jesus with a pretty good idea of what I want Him to do for me.

I like Os Guinness's definition of calling. He says that

"calling is the truth that God calls us to hir
that everything we are, everything we do,
have is invested with a special devotion a
out as a response to his summons and service. -

For Peter and Andrew, the call came on just another day while they went about their usual business of gathering fish. God often chooses ordinary life as the setting to call us to Himself. From that point on, their purpose in life became single-mindedly focused on the only one who mattered: Jesus Christ of Nazareth.

They went where He told them to go. They did what He told them to do. They listened when He spoke. And they were in for the ride of their lives.

Their lives became about Christ and for Christ, even though they knew little of Christ yet. Did they understand the full meaning of repentance from sin yet? Did they see the depth of their own sinfulness and their desperate need for a Savior yet? We may never know, but what we do know is that Peter and Andrew had responded to the call of Christ though they knew little of the stripping process that was to come.

Are you still looking for your purpose in life?

Everyone everywhere wants to know why. Why am I here? Why was I born?

People spend years trying to figure it out. They read books in the hopes of understanding the answer. They argue about it, they pontificate about it, they dream about it. It should come as no surprise to us that Rick Warren's *The Purpose Driven Life* became one of the bestselling books of all time. People simply want to know what the purpose of their life is.

The answer doesn't always come in the same way for everyone, but the answer is always the same. Peter and Andrew understood it one morning in Galilee when Jesus of Nazareth beckoned them to come follow Him.

I understood it one evening in Wisconsin when Christ's call got ahold of my life. I wasn't called to join a church, or a movement. The Savior Himself had called me, and turning back was never even an option. I was called to follow the One who had given me everything, and I was ready to give Him everything in return. I took a leap of faith and expected Christ to catch me. His arms were more than ready. They were held wide open for me on the cross. All I had to do was believe.

Have you responded to God's call in your life? His call is available to anyone who will answer it. Paul affirms it in Romans 10:13: "Everyone who calls on the name of the Lord will be saved." John asserts it in Revelation 3:20: "Behold, I stand at the door and knock. If anyone hears my voice and opens the door, I will come in to him and eat with him, and he with me."

It happened to Paul on the road to Damascus on a warm, sunny, Middle Eastern day. It happened to the Ethiopian eunuch in a carriage on the road to Gaza while reading Isaiah (Acts 8:26–39). And it can happen to you right now. This is a call you can't afford to miss. Will you open the door of your heart and invite the Savior in, or will you ignore His call and let it go to voice mail? This is the most important call of your life.

Maybe you're still having a hard time hearing His call. Let me tell you my favorite story in the Bible of God calling someone to Himself.

HERE I AM?

You may or may not be familiar with the story of Samuel. His mother's name was Hannah. She was a nice lady married to an interesting man named Elkanah. Elkanah had two wives, but he preferred Hannah. They were God-fearing people who worshiped God and went to church on a regular basis. But Hannah had a problem. She couldn't have children. This is a big deal anytime, but it was a really big deal back in Bible days. One year when the family went up to worship, Hannah was so distressed about her childlessness and became so moved in prayer that the priest thought she was drunk.

It's hard to believe that anyone can pray this fervently, but Hannah did. That year, God heard her prayer, and she became pregnant. She had a son.

The boy's name was Samuel.

If anyone was wired to hear God's call in his life, it should have been Samuel. He was a miracle boy. He grew up in God's house. He was prayed over. He was well-trained by a priest. But when the day came and God called him, Samuel didn't even recognize God's voice.

It was nighttime. Eli, Samuel's mentor, was already asleep. Samuel was lying down in his corner thinking about the events of the day when he heard his name. Here's what happened in 1 Samuel 3: "Then The Lord called Samuel, and he said 'Here I am!' and ran to Eli and said, 'Here I am, for you called me.' But he said, 'I did not call; lie down again.' So he went and lay down" (vv. 4–5).

To Eli, it sounded like Samuel was a kid trying to get out of going to sleep. This happened three times in a row. By the third time, Eli finally got a clue:

And the Lord called Samuel again the third time. And he arose and went to Eli and said, "Here I am, for you called me." Then Eli perceived that the Lord was calling the boy. Therefore Eli said to Samuel, "Go, lie down, and if he calls you, you shall say, 'Speak, Lord for your servant hears.'" So Samuel went and lay down in his place. And the Lord came and stood, calling as at other times, "Samuel! Samuel!" And Samuel said, "Speak, for your servant hears." (vv. 8–10)

Thus was born one of the greatest prophets of the entire Old Testament. Little did Samuel know in that moment that he would someday anoint not only the first king of Israel, Saul, but also the greatest king of Israel, a kid named David. Little did Samuel know what the future would hold for him. Little did he foresee the trials that would come and the stripping that would follow.

Do you, like Samuel, find it hard to recognize God's voice in your life? Has it been awhile since you've heard God speak?

A DIFFERENT KIND OF CALL

Let me give you four characteristics of God's call from the story of Samuel:

1. It's personal.

God didn't just yell out any name. He called Samuel personally. He used his name. You can almost sense the Lord cupping His hand over Samuel's ear and whispering the name. *Samuel. Samuel.* There's nothing quite like being called by your name, is there? You could be in a crowd full of people, but the minute someone calls you by name, your ears perk up, your hope builds up. For a moment, you feel known. You feel loved. That's how God's call comes to us.

2. *It's persistent.*

I can be quite dense and so focused on my life that I miss most calls the first time they come through. Once in a while, when I finally look at my phone, I'll see six missed calls from someone I love. That's what I call persistence. It's also a sign that there's a call I can't afford to miss. God called Samuel's name three different times. You get a sense that God would have kept calling until Samuel finally would have answered. God's love is that persistent.

3. *It's patient.*

When I miss several calls by the same person and I finally call back, I typically get an annoyed response on the other line: "Where have you been? Why didn't you answer?" For a moment, I almost regret calling back. God's call is nothing like that. He is patient and long-suffering, not willing that any should perish but that all should come to repentance (2 Peter 3:9). He is patient in His persistence, and it is this loving and steadfast patience that finally got a deep hold on Samuel's heart, causing him to respond. Has God's call gotten ahold of your heart yet? God is patiently waiting for you to answer.

4. *It's powerful.*

Once heeded, God's call is so powerful that nothing ever stays the same again. For Peter and Andrew, it meant throwing in their nets and following a carpenter named Jesus. For Samuel, it meant becoming the man who would confront his mentor, Eli, of the coming judgment on Eli's family because of their sinfulness. The moment you respond to God's call is the moment you will experience His powerful presence in your life, transforming you into Christ's likeness.

A CAVEAT

People often tell me that they regularly hear God audibly speak in their lives. I have a confession to make: I've never heard God speak audibly in my life. For years I used to think something was very wrong with me. I wondered why God would withhold His voice from my life. Was it something I did? Was it something I said?

Turns out that nothing is really wrong with me at all. If you've wondered whether you've missed God's call because you've never heard Him speak, you need to hear what I'm about to say: God's primary method of speaking to us today is through His Word. Listen to Romans 10:14–15, 17:

GOD CAN SPEAK anytime He wants to in any way He wants to.

How then will they call on him in whom they have not believed? And how are they to believe in him of whom they have never heard? And how are they to hear without someone preaching? And how are they to preach unless they are sent? As it is written, "How beautiful are the feet of those who preach the good news!" . . . So faith comes from hearing, and hearing through the word of Christ.

Let's get one thing straight: God can speak anytime He wants to in any way He wants to. He's God, after all. But according to this passage in Romans, He speaks to us primarily through His Word. God often uses other people to help us hear His Word. This happened to Samuel through Eli. It happened to the Ethiopian eunuch through Philip. It happened to the early church through the preaching of Peter and Paul.

It happened to me through people like my own mother who shared Christ with me as a child. It happened to me later on in my life through the preacher on that warm summer night at camp.

And for some of you hearing this stuff for the first time, it's happening to you right now through me. God is calling to you to Himself through His Word as I've explained it to you. You have just received the most important call of your life. What will you do with it? Will you respond to Jesus Christ who has given His life for you? Will you accept His invitation to set you free from your sin? Will you take a leap of faith and yield yourself to Him, trusting Him to save you?

In Romans 10:9–10, Paul tells us that "if you confess with your mouth that Jesus is Lord and believe in your heart that God raised him from the dead, you will be saved. For with the heart one believes and is justified, and with the mouth one confesses and is saved."

You may be wondering, *Saved from what?* The answer is well explained in *The Pilgrim's Progress.* Christian, the hero of the story, has just received "the call." He knows his life is missing something, but he does not know which direction to go. He runs into Evangelist, and the following conversation takes place:

Evangelist asked, "If this is your condition, why are you standing here?"

[Christian] replied, "Because I don't know where to go."

The Evangelist gave him a letter in which was written: "Flee from the coming wrath."

The man therefore read it and, looking very carefully upon Evangelist, asked, "Where must I flee?"

Then, pointing with his finger over a very wide field, Evangelist said, "Do you see that Narrow Gate over there?"

"No," replied the man.

Then the other asked, "Do you see that shining light there?"

"I think I do," answered the man.

Then Evangelist said, "Keep that light in your eye and go up directly toward it. Then you will see the Gate. When you knock on the Gate, you'll be told what you must do."

So in my dream I saw the man begin to run. He had not run far from his own door before his wife and children, having seen it, began to cry after him to return. But the man put his fingers in his ears and ran on, crying, "Life! Life! Eternal Life!" So, not turning to look behind him, he fled toward the middle of the plain.[2]

THE MINUTE we hit the wilderness, we panic and want to bolt.

Saved from wrath for eternal life. For the man or woman who has heard God's call and accepted it, these words bring fullness of joy and satisfaction that nothing can compare to.

All right. So you've answered God's call for salvation, but

does it end there? Is this all there is for the Christian?

Though most Christians intuitively understand the kind of life-altering call of Jesus Christ, many get stuck and never move beyond the practical application of what this call means. It's the reason why so many followers of Jesus Christ today seem to be wasting their lives instead of using them for God's glory.

Worse yet, many followers of Jesus Christ abandon ship at the merest sign of difficulty that creeps up along the narrow road of faith. Throughout the gospels, Christ warns the Christian of the difficult road ahead. Take these examples for instance:

- ♦ "For the gate is narrow and the way is hard that leads to life, and those who find it are few." Matthew 7:14.
- ♦ "If anyone would come after me, let him deny himself and take up his cross daily and follow me. For whoever would save his life will lose it, but whoever loses his life for my sake will save it." Luke 9:23–24.
- ♦ "In the world you will have tribulation. But take heart; I have overcome the world." John 16:33.

Though we're given ample warning of the difficult road ahead, most of us cower in fear at the earliest signs of discomfort.

We're a lot like the Israelites after they were called out of Egypt. We don't have trouble leaving Egypt, the land of slavery and defeat, but the minute we hit the wildernesss, we panic and want to bolt.

Their life was bad. Their days were long. All they wanted was to be freed from the bondage of slavery. They would have done anything to be free. They cried about it. They prayed about it. They sang about it. They waited hundreds of years for it.

Until one day, God saved them. He did it powerfully. He did it magnificently. He did it faithfully and lovingly through His servant Moses. You may have seen the movie with Charlton Heston in it. Or maybe you haven't.

It may surprise you, but instead of delivering them out of their slavery into a forty-year vacation, God led the Israelites straight out of Egypt into the wilderness. Yikes. What kind of God does that?

To say that the Israelites did not expect the wilderness is an understatement. The wilderness would strip the Israelites of everything, but it was God's perfect and purposed plan for His people. In Exodus 13:17–18, God gives us His perspective on it:

> When Pharaoh let the people go, God did not lead them by way of the land of the Philistines, although that was near. For God said, "Lest the people change their minds when they see war and return to Egypt." But God led the people around by the way of the wilderness toward the Red Sea. And the people of Israel went up out of the land of Egypt equipped for battle.

The Israelites should have seen it coming. But instead, they turned to complaining and fear. They turned to impatience and idolatry. We'll talk about them some more in the chapters to come. But more than anything, the Israelites missed two very critical facts.

The first was that the wilderness was part of God's call and plan. The wilderness was meant to make the Israelites stronger. It was meant to make them leaner, and better able to fight the battles that God had for them. The wilderness was a time of preparation and a time of purification. The wilderness was the perfect place for the Israelites to become God's people. *The second fact that the Israelites missed was that God was with them every step of the way through the wilderness.* For the Israelites, God's presence was obvious through a pillar of cloud by day and a pillar of fire by night.

God's plan is the same for His children today. He starts by calling us to Himself. The rest of our life is a journey to become more like Him. It is a journey toward a deeper knowledge of Him and a closer walk with Him. It is a journey into life. If you're a seasoned Christian, you're probably familiar with the word *sanctification* that God uses for this process. I like the word *stripping*. I like it because admittedly, the wilderness does not always feel like a perfect place. It's often a place of pain, and a place of endurance, and a place of doubt. How could the loving Savior who called us out of Egypt really mean for us to last in the oppressive heat and dangers of the wilderness? Could this really be part of His plan for us?

ADMITTEDLY, THE wilderness does not always feel like the perfect place.

If you're like me, you've probably wondered why the wilderness is necessary. If you're like me, you've probably been tempted to escape. If you're like me, you've wished for a pillar of fire to guide you when the night is dark. The irony is that just like the Israelites we have been given a pillar, but we have lost sight of it more often than we can imagine. Our pillar of fire is God's Word. He is our presence in the darkest wilderness. He is our guide when the storms come as they most certainly will. Throughout the next chapters, I'm going to walk you through the stripping process that every single Christian must go through in response to God's call. I'm going to spend some time talking about how to survive the stripping process. I'm also going to help you move past the pain of being stripped and find joy in the midst of the wilderness.

Many Christians have a life verse. I happen to have one too. It's Philippians 1:6. It goes like this: "And I am sure of this, that he who began a good work in you will bring it to completion at the day of Jesus Christ." This verse is a summary of what this book is about. God is up to something. He who called us is faithful and will complete the work He's started. God's promise to us is that no matter how painful the road we're on may seem, the end is sure and secure.

Look, I've answered many calls in my life: the call to personal purity, the call to full-time ministry, the call to start a blog and to write a book and to lead the women's ministry at my church. Each season in my life has been unique in its own right, but none can compare to the most important call in my life that undergirds all others: the call to follow Jesus Christ as my Lord and Savior.

Why is it that some Christians hear God's call better than others do?

Let's consider the prophet Habakkuk for the answer.

Habakkuk was a prophet who lived in a time when things weren't looking very good. The culture was bad. The people had deviated from God's ways. No one seemed to know what to do or how to fix it. Habakkuk was pretty depressed about it. He couldn't figure out why God wouldn't just do something and fix it. He was so depressed that he prayed. Unbelievably, God answered. Here's how the conversation went.

"I will take my stand at my watchpost and station myself on the tower, and look out to see what he will say to me, and what I will answer concerning my complaint. And the Lord answered me: 'Write the vision; make it plain on tablets, so he may run who reads it' " (Habakkuk 2:1–2).

We live in a day of vision-seeking and vision-claiming. There are hundreds if not thousands of books on how to develop vision in your life and where to get more vision. God has a way of keeping things simple in life. You want answers in your life? Easy. Just ask Him for answers. The answers are in His Word. They have been written on tablets and saved through the ages for you.

If you're a Christian without a sense of purpose in your life, perhaps it's because you've never asked God what He wants to do with your life. Perhaps you've never hungered to know His plan for you. According to Ephesians 2:10, God created you for good works that He's prepared before for you to do before the world began!

WHAT KEEPS YOU FROM HEARING THE CALL

Besides not asking God for His will for your life, I believe there are four major obstacles to hearing God's call in your life.

1. *You are distracted by lesser things.*

We're living in a time of cultural ADHD. The options for our distraction are limitless and time consuming. You can lump any amount of entertainment options in this category of lesser things. It used to be simply the television, but we now can proudly add the Internet, Facebook, Twitter, video games, Netflix, Hulu, Apple TV, and on and on the list goes. No matter how good your intentions are, until you actively unplug the distractions in our life and simplify things, you will find that hearing God's voice will remain one of the greatest challenges of your life.

2. *You are divided by other relationships.*

The most well-meaning people in your life can stand in the way of God's call for you. It takes a deep sense of conviction to maintain a vertical focus when those closest to you try to dissuade you from pursuing God's call for your life. No matter your background and upbringing, chances are that your life is consumed by other relationships, some good, some not so good, that are keeping you from clearly hearing God's voice. Listening to God's voice in your life is a solo sport. It demands your full attention and devotion.

3. *You are discouraged by Satan's ploys.*

Satan takes great joy in discouraging Christ's followers. He does it through tempting you to sin. He does it through discouragement and doubt. He does it daily. He does it deceptively. But he does it as you allow him to. God has already overcome Satan and given us victory over him, but until you open your eyes and recognize Christ's victory in your life, you will remain pummeled by Satan's ploys. I pray the next chapters will give you the ammunition you need to win the battle against him.

4. *You are deceived by your pride.*

I have dedicated a whole chapter to discussing pride and how it keeps us from the abundant life in Christ. God is committed to stripping us of our pride until we are fully dependent on Him. I've had to learn this lesson the hard way, and I hope my own experience will encourage you to humbly turn to the Lord in absolute surrender and complete yieldedness.

Sometimes when I'm in the middle of a conversation, the cell phone reception gets fuzzy. When that happens to me, I'll walk around the room looking for a better location, and I'll ask the obvious question: "Can you hear me now?"

If you're having a hard time connecting with the Lord, it's not because He's not calling. Perhaps you simply need to get more familiar with His voice. It may be time for you to change

GOD IS COMMITTED to stripping us of our pride until we are fully dependent on Him.

your location, and like Samuel, answer the Lord with these words: "Speak Lord, for your servant hears."

When you do, you'd better believe He's going to answer. But be careful. The answer may not be quite what you're expecting. The answer to God's call is usually the beginning of the road to being stripped of all you find comfortable and safe.

Whether your calling today is to be the best mom you can be to your toddlers, or to glorify God as a single professional in the midst of a bustling city, or whether your calling today is in full-time ministry, I hope you're ready to hang on for dear life as you enjoy the ride in pursuit of the Savior.

You're going to find Him worth every bit of pain you feel in the process.

Almost six years ago I lost my relationship with both of my teenage sons because of my sinful response to my difficult marriage. I cried out to God daily and at times hourly to show me who I was since I was no longer a wife and a mother.

My life no longer appeared to have direction or definition. I was stripped bare and exposed. His answer was gentle but firm: Follow Me. Rest in Me. Know My grace.

I still grieve, but now with the Lord at my side. Today one relationship is restored but the other remains estranged. Today I know who I am in Christ. More importantly I know that He is enough and that He is with me in the waiting.

—SHERRY

Part Two

SURVIVING THE STRIPPING PROCESS

Chapter Two

ARE WE THERE YET?

Teach us, O Lord, the disciplines of patience, for to wait is often harder than to work. —PETER MARSHALL

People often ask me why I chose to practice emergency medicine. The answer is easy. I hate waiting. If there is one word in the English language that I cannot stand, it's the word *wait*.

I don't like anything about it. I don't like standing still. I don't like not knowing exactly when something is going to happen. I don't like idle instability and open-ended sentences. I am a fix-it, get-'er-done kind of person through and through.

I hate waiting so much that I'd rather resuscitate people than spend another minute in the waiting room. I hate waiting so much, I'd rather be quickly seated at Denny's than grab a buzzing square at a hipper restaurant. I hate waiting so much, I'd rather hang up on the customer service rep than get my money back on a big-ticket item.

If you look up the word *waiting* in a dictionary, you'll find synonyms like *a period of waiting, a pause, an interval,* or *a delay.* If you think I hate waiting, let me tell you what I think is even worse than waiting: delays. Anyone who has ever traveled anywhere with a toddler understands the frustration of a delay. It's horrific. It's painful. It's inevitable.

So I find it ironic that God not only uses delays in our lives, but purposefully orchestrates them as part of His master

41

plan to shape us into His likeness. Make a mental list of the men and women that God has used mightily for His glory and you will find yourself staring at a list of folks who became experts in delays and waiting.

There's Abraham who waited until he was one hundred years old to have his promised son Isaac. There's Joseph who waited for years until God finally broke open the door of his prison cell to use him. Then there's Moses who waited for forty years in the wilderness to live out God's call for him, and David who waited forever in the stronghold before he became king. Even Samson waited until his hair grew back before he could accomplish the job that God had called him to.

WAITING AN HOUR for your doctor can stretch your patience, but try waiting for forty years in a wilderness.

If you think the biblical examples are the only ones we have, you're wrong. For years my friend Beth believed God would give her a child. Instead of a baby, God has allowed Beth to go through thirteen miscarriages. Lisa, a friend of mine in full-time ministry, believes God has called her to be a mother to a Haitian orphan girl. She has pursued adoption plans but has faced several obstacles along the way. The adoption Lisa believed would happen in obedience to God's call has turned into an agonizing time of waiting while governmental bureaucracy drags on. Yes, waiting is part of God's great plan for you and me, yet nothing seems more painful to us than the agony of waiting.

Why is waiting part of God's perfect plan?

If I were forced to pick favorites, I'd still choose the Israelites as my poster people for waiting. Waiting for an hour for your doctor can stretch your patience, but try waiting for forty years in a wilderness until you reach the Promised Land. Whoa, Nelly.

I've already introduced you to the Israelites in the last chapter so you should know the basics. They were slaves in Egypt until God called them out of their place of bondage. They assumed the tough days were behind them, and were more than a little surprised when they found themselves trudging through the wilderness day after agonizingly long day.

It seems counterintuitive that God would go to such great lengths to deliver His people, only to have them land in a wilderness of waiting for forty long and painful years. Couldn't the God who saved Israel now make the way easy for them? Couldn't the God who parted the Red Sea snap His fingers and make something happen?

To be honest with you, it's easy for me to sympathize with the people of Israel. When I answered God's call to leave my Egypt, I had great dreams of the life ahead. I bet you did too. I packed my meager bags and got ready to hit the road. I looked forward to the better life ahead. With God on my side, what could go wrong?

A lot, apparently. When life suddenly comes to a screeching halt and the wilderness threatens to undo us, we look up and begin to question God. We quickly get tired of the same old manna. We feel parched but can't find any water to drink. Our questions turn to frustration and anger. Did God really call me out of Egypt? Or did I take a wrong turn somewhere?

Has God forgotten me? Was I imagining His call? Will the waiting ever end? Dreams remain unfulfilled. Prayers go un-answered. The silence overwhelms us. A blanket of confusion is our only comfort.

Once in a while on a busy shift in the ER, I'll walk into a room and the patient will greet me like this: "Hey, Doc, I thought you forgot about me." I chuckle. Little do the pa-tients know that back in my corner where I spend most of my time is a computer. On the computer is the exact location of every patient in the ER. I know when they walked in. I know where they're sitting. I know exactly how long it's been that they've been waiting for me. I also know something that would set my patients free if they knew it too:

When there is a delay, there's always a really good reason for it.

When the waiting gets tedious and I catch myself feeling forgotten by God, I make myself stop and I remember this truth: if God has delayed in answering, then there must be a reason for it.

REASONS FOR THE WAITING

I believe there are four specific reasons why God allows His children to wait.

1. The waiting is meant to grow us.

The people of Israel had a minor problem. They had spent their whole lives being slaves and were now called to be warriors. They barely knew how to hold a spear, let alone aim it correctly and hit their mark. God was aware of this weakness that the Israelites had, and it was not actually so

44

minor. The people of Israel were not aware of it. Remember the passage we looked at in Exodus 13:17–18:

> When Pharaoh let the people go, God did not lead them by way of the land of the Philistines, although that was near. For God said, "Lest the people change their minds when they see war and return to Egypt." But God led the people around by the way of the wilderness toward the Red Sea. And the people of Israel went up out of the land of Egypt equipped for battle.

In other words, God purposefully sent His people the long way to the Promised Land, not because He didn't care for them but because He knew what they did not know: their capacity to fight the enemy was still limited. They needed to get stronger. They needed to learn how to fight. They needed to become a strong nation that would override the enemy to claim the Promised Land.

I usually think I know all the answers to my life problems. I get frustrated when God doesn't cooperate by giving me what I want, when I want it. Do you ever feel that way? When God called me to a life in full-time ministry, I thought that accepting His call was the biggest step of faith I'd ever take. I naively expected God to

DIDN'T GOD want me to succeed?

"make it all happen" for me right there and then. So when the Christian blog that I started for God's glory didn't explode and reach thousands of readers by its first year, I was puzzled. Didn't God want me to succeed? And when the Bible study that I was teaching didn't catch fire, I accused God of messing with my mind. *Didn't You want me to be in full-time ministry? Wasn't this Your idea? What's with the waiting? Why the delays?* I couldn't see then what I clearly see now: the day that God called me into a life of ministry, I still wasn't ready to receive all that God had for me. I had to grow into the job that God was fitting me for. I had to learn how to write. I had to learn how to teach God's Word.

What I forgot in the waiting is that God is the Potter and I am the clay. He's the one who is shaping me and reworking me into the perfect vessel for His use. All I have to do is trust Him to finish the work in His time.

2. The waiting is meant to protect us.

Read what Deuteronomy 7:22 says: "The Lord your God will clear away these nations before you little by little. You may not make an end of them at once, lest the wild beasts grow too numerous for you."

Wait. Wild beasts? I thought the enemy nations were the only obstacle the people of Israel had to worry about. Who said anything about wild beasts?

Here's something you need to know: God makes a habit of protecting us from dangers we haven't even imagined or predicted.

A few years ago I was ready to change jobs. I knew God had called me to full-time ministry, but I was still working in an academic medical center with its rigors and demands. I was anxious to move on. I had a blog that was growing, and I was teaching more and more Bible studies in one of the largest churches in the United States. Instead of worrying about medical grants, I wanted to focus on Bible study facts. I was in a rush to get there.

For two years I thought about changing jobs until one day I took action. I heard about an opportunity across town that sounded perfect. I applied for it, but the door slammed in my face so hard I can still feel its impact. How could God allow this to happen to me? The next three months were uneventful. I waited. Then one day, out of the random blue, I got a call. It was from a third hospital across town where some of my friends worked. A position had become available. The call was unexpected; I hadn't gone looking for it, but the job was perfect for me. The pay was higher, the hours less than anything I'd heard of before, and my partners were idyllic. I couldn't have crafted a better fit for me if I'd tried. That job would allow me to transition into the women's ministry director role at my church because of its flexibility. Ironically, I would later be given the chance to moonlight at the hospital where the door had slammed shut in my face. It turned out that I hated working at that hospital. Every shift that I worked there was a reminder to me of God's grace in my life. Every shift that I spent there was a reminder that God knows what I need far more than I do.

God never makes mistakes. He knows what's best for His children. And He sometimes allows us to spend time in the wilderness of waiting for our own protection. Won't you trust Him in your season of waiting?

3. *The waiting is meant to test us.*

So far we've talked about how God uses the waiting to grow our faith, and to protect us from unseen dangers. In

Deuteronomy 8:2 we're given the third reason for waiting.

"And you shall remember the whole way that the Lord your God has led you these forty years in the wilderness, that he might humble you, testing you to know what was in your heart, whether you would keep his commandments or not."

I've taken enough tests in my life to know that I don't like them. Yet God often uses the delays in our life to test us. He uses the waiting to see if we will lean on Him in complete dependence or if we will choose our own wisdom instead. The Bible often uses the imagery of refining silver as an example of the way God tests us. In Zechariah 13:9 it says: "And I will put this third into the fire, and refine them as one refines silver, and test them as gold is tested."

Refining silver is not easy. It's fierce work. It involves beating the silver and hammering it in the perfect places to make it as pure and refined as possible. It's work that takes time. It's work that involves the searing pain of fire. It's work that will test you until you feel like you're going to crack.

ASK YOURSELF whether it is your own sin that is keeping you in the land of waiting.

But under the skillful loving hand of the Master, cracking is never a risk. God's plan is not to crack us but to test us.

Remember Peter, the fisherman turned fisher of men? He understood the importance of testing on the road to living out God's call. Here's what he tells us about it in 1 Peter 1:7: "So that the tested genuineness of your faith—more precious than gold that perishes though it is tested by fire—may be found to result in praise and glory and honor at the revelation of Jesus Christ."

Waiting is a test that every follower of Jesus Christ will have to take over and over again. I hope you're passing it.

4. *The waiting is meant to purify us.*

Once in a while, the waiting in our life is extended because of our own sinfulness. Malachi 3:2–3 explains this kind of waiting: "For he is like a refiner's fire and like fullers' soap. He will sit as a refiner and purifier of silver, and he will purify the sons of Levi and refine them like gold and silver, and they will bring offerings in righteousness to the Lord."

God's Word in Ezekiel 22:19–20 is even stronger: "Because you have all become dross, therefore, behold, I will gather you into the midst of Jerusalem. As one gathers silver and bronze and iron and lead and tin into a furnace, to blow the fire on it in order to melt it, so I will gather you in my anger and in my wrath, and I will put you in and melt you."

Ouch.

Sadly, the Israelites became well-versed in the purification process. The Israelites could have entered the Promised Land earlier on in their journey, but their own sin in the wilderness prolonged their waiting from a long weekend to an extended-stay vacation. As you consider your own life, ask yourself whether it is your own sin that is keeping you in the land of waiting.

I'm so grateful for God's commitment to my purification. I'm so thankful that He won't allow the dross to accumulate in my life. But I've often wondered how much of my time in the wilderness has been caused by my own sin and stubbornness?

This is a great time to discuss the common temptations we face in times of waiting with the hope that we will avoid falling prey to them.

TEMPTATIONS WE FACE IN THE WAITING

Let's review a bit. God called the people of Israel out of Egypt. They were to go to the Promised Land. They soon hit the wilderness. The wilderness was there for a reason. It was meant to make them stronger and to protect them. It was meant to test them and to grow their faith. It was a time of purification.

But instead of seeing God's provision for them in the waiting, all the Israelites could see was the tragedy of their plight. Instead of being thankful for God's presence along the way, all they could do was focus on what they thought were horrible circumstances. Instead of looking upward to the pillar of fire, they looked inward at their own unmet cravings.

They just didn't get it.

By the time we get to Exodus 32, we have a pretty good idea of the kind of people these guys were. They were fickle, fair-weather people. They didn't deserve God's goodness, yet God never gave up on them. He had made an unconditional promise to Abraham and to Isaac and to Jacob and He was committed to the people He had called to Himself.

One day, Moses went up on the mountain for an extended meeting with God. The meeting lasted forty days, but for the people of Israel it felt like a lifetime. Here's how it rolled in Exodus 32:1:

When the people saw that Moses delayed to come down from the mountain, the people gathered themselves together to Aaron and said to him, "Up, make us gods who shall go before us. As for this Moses, the man who brought us up out of the land of Egypt, we do not know what has become of him."

Wait. What just happened? The people of Israel, tired of waiting on God, made four drastic mistakes giving us a perfect example of what not to do when delays come our way.

1. Don't take matters into your own hands.

Tired of waiting for Moses to come back, the people of Israel figured they didn't need God or Moses. They could make things happen on their own. If you've ever tried this before, you know that it's not a great plan.

When I first became the women's ministry director at my church, I had a huge learning curve ahead. Though I knew the position was part of God's call on my life, I had a hard time adjusting to church life. I was an ER doctor used to getting what I wanted, when I wanted it. I was the boss, and everyone does what the doctor orders. Turns out, it doesn't work that way in the real world. One particular month, things got pretty bad. I prayed. When God didn't answer me in a minute, I decided to take matters into my own hands.

I quit.

I really did. It was dumb. It was selfish. But I did it. At first, I felt vindicated. I'd showed them who was boss. I woke up the next morning and realized that I'd just made the biggest mistake of my life. God had called me to a life in ministry

> CHOOSING TO take matters into your own hands, when God has called you to wait, is a big deal.

but the moment things didn't go my way, I bailed. I was really doing a great job of proving to God that I was the right candidate for His work. Yeah, right.

When the Israelites decided to take matters into their own hands, things didn't turn out well for them. By the end of that day, 23,000 of them would die.

By God's grace, my suffering was small compared to the Israelites. My job was restored, but I had to learn some humbling lessons in the process. I was beginning to learn a critical lesson that every follower of Christ must learn: choosing to take matters into your own hands, when God has called you to wait, is a big deal. Waiting for Him to act will always yield joy.

2. Don't turn to others for approval.

Let me tell you about the man named Aaron. He was the head priest, God's guy. He was Moses's brother, and he'd been around since the beginning. He had seen all God had done for Israel up close and personal. God had used him mightily. Moses trusted him. The people respected him. But when faced with a delay, Aaron did what we're all tempted to do when faced with the same situation.

He looked to others for approval. He valued people's opinions more than he honored God's. He caved to the pressures around him instead of standing strong in the Lord. The people of Israel offered to put him on a bit of a pedestal. They made him feel more important than he really was. And he fell for it hook, line, and sinker. The next thing you know, Aaron was making a golden calf for the people of Israel in a desperate effort to please them.

How easily swayed by public opinion we are. Instead of turning to the Lord for approval and for the answers we need, we take public opinion surveys and poll everyone we know on how we ought to behave. We neglect God's Word and its absolute authority in our lives, and we choose to impress others instead.

Whose opinion is most important to you? Who are you seeking to please in your life?

3. Don't turn to idols for comfort.

The golden calf incident brought the demise of many of the people of Israel. It caused them death. It separated them from God. It delayed them from entering the Promised Land. It would necessitate a mediator and their heartfelt repentance.

It's easy to turn to idols for comfort during times of prolonged waiting. If God doesn't provide what we think we need, we'll find a way to get it without His help.

I've been single a long, long time. I know all about the waiting. I waited forever for my first date. I waited even longer for my first kiss. And I'm still waiting for my happily ever after. At one point in my life, I felt like I'd waited long enough for the Lord to provide a perfect man for me. When He didn't, I was hurt. Didn't God think I was good enough to get married? Didn't He care about me? Soon my hurt turned to resentment. Could I trust this God who created me with a desire for marriage but didn't make provision for my need? It didn't take long for my resentment to turn to sin. Instead of turning to the Lord with my need, I chose to turn to my own idols for comfort. After a while, no matter how hard I tried, it seemed I couldn't get victory over certain sins in my life.

The worst part of my story is that I blamed God for my sin. I was miserable. I was broken. Was this the life that God had called me to? If the cross of Jesus was supposed to change everything, how come it wasn't changing me? Why did I find more satisfaction in my idols than I did in the Lord? Had I missed some basic link in Christianity? What was happening to me?

COULD I TRUST this God who created me with a desire for marriage but didn't make provision for my need?

It took me a long time to understand a very basic step in gaining victory over besetting sins and idolatry in my life. Only God will satisfy me completely, but the only way to get rid of the idols in my life is to destroy them completely and make room for the Lord instead.

In Exodus 32:20 when Moses came down from his mountain meeting with the Lord, it says that "he took the calf that they had made and burned it with fire and ground it to powder and scattered it on the water and made the people of Israel drink it."

There is no other way of dealing with your idols than to utterly and completely destroy them. You can't negotiate your way out of them. You can't keep on justifying them. You can't over-intellectualize them or ignore them or bury them.

If you long for freedom more than you long for anything

else in your life, you simply must take an initial step of faith and kill your idols. Take a hammer and destroy them. Throw them in the fire. Burn away the dross. Fall on your knees in repentance and ask God for mercy.

He always gives it. He's provided a mediator, Jesus Christ, who's already paid the price for your freedom. In your time of waiting, let Him be your joy instead of turning to your idols for comfort. He's the only one who can fully satisfy you.

4. Don't tell yourself lies about your circumstances.

The people of Israel told themselves lies about their circumstances. When they looked for Moses and didn't find him, they told each other that Moses was gone forever. They convinced themselves that the only way out was to do it their own way, and they turned their lives into one huge disaster. They believed the lie that God didn't care about them and had forgotten them.

When I'm in the wilderness of waiting, it's easy for me to tell myself lies about my own circumstances: God has forgotten me. He doesn't care about me. If He really wanted me here, life wouldn't be so hard. If His call was for real, I wouldn't feel so weak.

I begin to doubt His love, and I question His promises. I wonder about His goodness. Can God truly be trusted?

Nothing will steal the Christian's joy like believing lies about God. It's blasphemous and destructive. We must learn to replace the lies with God's truth.

Do you want to know the worst part about the disaster in the wilderness? In the very last verse of Exodus 31, right before the people of Israel gave up on Moses and decided he wasn't coming back to the camp, we're told: "And [God] gave to Moses, when he had finished speaking with him on Mount Sinai, the two tablets of the testimony, tablets of stone, written with the finger of God" (v. 18).

In other words, it was literally minutes before the golden calf incident that Moses was headed back to the camp armed with the tablets from God. The waiting was just about over.

If only the people of Israel had been willing to patiently wait just one more day in the wilderness. If only they hadn't given up. If only . . .

What wilderness are you going through right now? Are you tempted to give up? Has the waiting gone too long? Are you tempted to take matters into your own hands and escape the waiting that God has trusted you with?

Consider this: there is another way. It's the way of waiting well. Do you want to learn it?

HOW TO WAIT WELL

God had given a vision for Habakkuk's life. I guess you can call it a calling. It will fill you with joy to know that God has called you to do something special for Him. Most of us grab on to that and want to go all out for God in order to fulfill His calling in our life. We feel special. We want to see Him do something bigger than us.

The problem is that we can't accomplish spiritual goals without spiritual strategies, and spiritual strategies typically involve waiting. Here's what Habakkuk 2:3 says: "For still the vision awaits its appointed time; it hastens to the end—it will not lie. If it seems slow, wait for it; it will surely come; it will not delay."

That's good news and that's bad news, my friend.

It's bad news if you don't like waiting because God's promise to us is that pursuing His calling is a definite time of waiting. Unfortunately, because we as Christ's followers often misunderstand the reasons for the waiting season, doubts and fears arise. Though I've rushed God more times than I can think, by God's grace I'm also learning how to wait well.

1. You need to wait on His promises.

Here's a fact: God's promises will always come to pass. Every one of the words He has spoken will take place. God is always true. He is always faithful. Despite all of Israel's sin, God still remained true to His promise to Abraham and was faithful even to the stiff-necked people of Israel. He's incredible that way.

When I was sixteen God gave me a promise: He who began a good work in me would complete it in Jesus Christ. I didn't know how He would get it done, but I was given the promise that He would. It doesn't matter how long God wants me to wait or how many delays come my way, God will remain true to His promise.

God has given me many other promises since that day. He's promised to set me apart for the works that He has planned for me. He's promised to anoint me to bring good news to the poor. He's promised to go with me wherever He commands me to go. He's promised to forgive me when I repent, and He's promised that I am not condemned in Christ. He's given you those exact same promises too!

We don't always have all the details, but we do have all of

IT DOESN'T MATTER how long God wants me to wait or how many delays come my way, God will remain true to His promises.

God's promises. God's Word is what we can hang on to when our circumstances look uncertain. God's Word is our hope when our feelings are erratic. God's Word is our stability in time of trouble. His Word is our hope in the wilderness. His Word is our security when we don't have the answers. His Word is our rest in the monotonous drudgery of the waiting.

Are you becoming more and more familiar with God's Word in your life? Do you spend time in His Word? Do you pore over it and ask God to speak to you through His Word? Maybe it's time to start so that when the waiting comes, you have a solid place to pitch your tent and dwell on the faithfulness of God's promises!

2. You need to wait in His presence.

One of the scariest chapters in the life of the people of Israel came right after the golden calf incident. I've already told you that 23,000 people died on that day. What's even worse than this tragedy is that immediately following the plague, God sent the people of Israel off into the wilderness with an angel as their guide.

Up until that point, God had been their guide. This was horrible news for the Israelites and for Moses. Here's how God said it in Exodus 33:3, "but I will not go up among you, lest I consume you on the way, for you are a stiff-necked people."

God was going to remove His presence from the people of Israel. The people of Israel freaked out. It says in Exodus 33:4 that "when the people heard this disastrous word, they mourned, and no one put on his ornaments."

For Moses, it wasn't even an option. In Exodus 33:12–23 Moses summed up his perspective on the situation like this: God, if You don't lead me, if You don't go with me, I'm not going anywhere. I'd rather die than go without You.

Have you gotten to the place in your life where life isn't even imaginable or possible without God's manifest presence? The key to enjoying God's manifest presence is a total and complete turning away from your sin. Are you living the kind of life that welcomes God's manifest presence, or are you stubbornly holding on to your sin?

It is only in the Lord's presence that the wilderness of waiting becomes a place of great comfort. Are you willing to do whatever it takes to remain in His presence? His presence, after all, is the safest place to live.

3. *You need to wait for Him patiently.*

When we started this chapter I confessed to you that I don't like waiting. As an ER doctor, one of the worst things to wait for is the lab. No matter when the lab gets the specimen, the answer I get when I call them is that it's going to take five minutes more for the results to come back. Seriously?

Waiting on God can feel a little bit like waiting on lab results. It always seems to take just five minutes more than we have. Most of us are low on patience. And it feels like forever before we see any results. How long are you willing to wait on the Lord? Isaiah 64:4 says: "From of old no one has heard or perceived by the ear, no eye has seen a God besides you, who acts for those who wait for him." God doesn't ignore His children. He isn't oblivious to our waiting.

He is good. He knows what we need. He sees every bend in the road. He knows every bump on the way. His delays are for our good. He's like a good father who won't let his seven-year-old get behind the wheel, because, well, it's not time to drive yet. He's like the mother of a thirteen-year-old girl who reminds her daughter that it's too early to give your heart away, lest it get broken. God knows that there's a perfect time and a perfect season for everything. He makes everything beautiful in its time.

> **GOD, IF YOU** don't lead me, if You don't go with me, I'm not going anywhere.

God hasn't forgotten you. He isn't busy solving other people's problems while neglecting yours. He is always perfecting that which concerns your life. He loves you.

I told you that there's good news and bad news about waiting on God. I've already given you the bad news. But I think it's time for some good news. Maybe you missed the second half of Habakkuk 2:3. Here's what it says: "If it seems slow, wait for it; it will surely come; it will not delay."

The good news is that the waiting will end! Before you know it, the stripping will be over, the wilderness days will be in your rearview mirror, and fullness of joy will be yours.

In the next chapter, we're going to talk about one of the most critical things that God wants to strip His children of. I'm talking about pride.

My husband and I led worship for twenty-five years until we had to step down because of a sin issue he needed freedom from.

I became angry and insecure. I realized that I had wrapped my whole identity in my position as a worship leader. I felt very insignificant in the church since I had derived my status from my position as a worship leader. By stripping away our ministry, God was dealing with my pride and teaching me to find my identity in Him alone.

Today we are still waiting to see how God will use us and what the future will hold. But today, I know who I am in Christ and I am so grateful just to be His child.

—NANCY

Chapter Three

I'M TOO SEXY FOR MY SHIRT

I have had more troubles with myself than with any other man. —D. L. MOODY

Proud people generally don't think they're proud. I know because I was one of them for the longest time.

There was a time in my life when I felt as if God had finally hit the jackpot by gaining me as a follower. I was young. I was sold out. I was smart enough, pretty enough, funny enough, and I wanted to save the world.

I remember thinking that God also got Himself a bunch of added bonuses in the deal. I spoke three languages fluently, so I could go anywhere for Him. I was going to be a doctor, so I could do anything for Him. I was easygoing and flexible. And I was single. I had nothing better to do with my time than to serve Him. God was so lucky to have me.

Yeah. It wasn't pretty.

It didn't take long for me to realize that what I thought were assets that God had "gained" were more like hindrances that stood in the way of me being used by God in the way that He longed to use me. God had a lot of work left to do in my life.

In Habakkuk 2:3 we saw how God's call is usually followed by a season of waiting. Interestingly, in the very next verse God talks about pride. Here's what He says: "Behold, his soul is puffed up; it is not upright within him, but the righteous shall live by his faith" (v. 4).

It seems jarring to go from a discussion on waiting to the topic of pride. The context, however, is clearer than you initially catch. What God is saying is that faith requires humility, and that the only way to survive the waiting process is by resting completely in the Lord and refusing to trust your own wiles. In other words, God has to strip us of our pride in order for us to survive the waiting process in utter dependence on Him.

Ironically, God has given us plenty of biblical examples of pride to forewarn us about its wickedness, but most of us are too proud to see it. Satan himself used to be an angel of light until pride took over and he became God's greatest enemy. His story is told in Isaiah 14:12–16:

> How you are fallen from heaven, O Day Star, son of Dawn! How you are cut down to the ground, you who laid the nations low! You said in your heart, "I will ascend to heaven; above the stars of God I will set my throne on high; I will sit on the mount of assembly in the far reaches of the north; I will ascend above the heights of the clouds; I will make myself like the Most High." But you are brought down to Sheol, to the far reaches of the pit. Those who see you will stare at you and ponder over you.

How sad his story is. How pathetic and wasted Satan's life turned out to be.

The stories of pride unfortunately don't stop with Satan. There was Adam and Eve who chose to trust their gut instead of listening to God's good command. There was Cain who, in his pride, refused to accept God's correction and spent his days wandering

GOD WAS SO lucky to have me.

apart from the Lord. Then there's Lot who said, "Me, me, me," when standing at the crossroads of his life. The Israelites had to spend forty years in the wilderness getting to the end of themselves.

You get the picture. God hates pride. Pride has kept people from God, and it has prevented people from seeing the truth clearly. Pride has brought people down and hindered their growth and potential. Pride has destroyed nations for centuries, and pride continues to be a personal threat to you and me.

But the person I'd like us to home in on as we look at how pride reveals itself in the life of the follower of Jesus Christ is none other than stupid Samson.

THE BEST EXAMPLE OF PRIDE IN THE BIBLE

I hope you're not offended by my calling Samson stupid, but let me tell you a little more about Samson and you may find yourself agreeing with my assessment.

His life started out on a high note. His parents couldn't have kids, but after a season of praying and waiting, God eventually granted their prayer request. Not only did God give Manoah and his wife a son, but He made them a pretty big promise. Listen to Judges 13:3–5:

Behold, you are barren and have not borne children, but you shall conceive and bear a son. Therefore be careful and drink no wine or strong drink, and eat nothing unclean, for behold, you shall conceive and bear a son. No razor shall come upon his head, for the child shall be a Nazirite to God from the womb, and he shall begin to save Israel from the hand of the Philistines.

Wow. Talk about a calling. God promised this barren couple that their son, Samson, would save the people of Israel on the condition that he would never spend a dime on a haircut. It doesn't get much easier than that.

The parents believed God's promise. They taught their son all about God's ways and the importance of fearing the Lord. Who would have predicted that Samson's head would get so big, not with the fullness of his mane, but with the bloating of his pride?

Instead of believing God's promises, Samson soon started believing his own press. Instead of waiting on God's timing, Samson decided to take his life in his own hands. How tragic for Samson, yet how familiar to you and me.

How could Samson miss the impending disaster in his life when it seems so obvious to us reading his story today? In much the same way, many of us find ourselves sinking by the weight of our own pride, on the verge of our own disasters. Our only hope is that Christ would strip us of our pride and restore us to Himself. Before we talk about how He does that, let me give you four ways that pride reveals itself in the life of the believer.

1. "I can handle this myself": the deception of self-dependence.

God's Word was clear in the days of Samson: don't marry a Philistine. It should have been easy to avoid disaster. But instead of listening to God, Samson figured he was strong enough to manage his own life his own way. He was, after all, the man with the mane. He didn't need God to interfere when it came to who he dated and who he chose to marry.

It wasn't long before Samson's self-reliance would get him into the land of the Philistines and married to a daughter of the Philistines. Samson's first marriage turned into a disaster, and he still didn't understand the full effect of his disobedience. Things went from bad to worse for Samson. His "handling his life his own way" eventually landed him in the clutches of the infamous Delilah who would seduce him to his demise.

Self-reliance is easy to be guilty of in our Western world where everyone tells us that we're strong enough to manage on our own. Pull yourself up by your britches. Work harder. Hustle. You can do it.

But God's Word is clear: "Trust in the Lord with all your heart, and do not lean on your own understanding. In all your ways acknowledge him, and he will make straight your paths" (Proverbs 3:5–6). You can't handle it yourself. Only complete dependence on the Lord will lead you to spiritual maturity and allow you to be used by God to fulfill His calling in your life. It's only as you let go of your plans and trust His that you will find full freedom and lasting joy.

2. "I deserve even more": the lie of self-righteousness.

There is an incident in Samson's life that is worth mentioning. Samson was headed down to Timnah to check out his newest Philistine crush. He came across a lion along the way. The Bible says that in that moment, "The Spirit of the Lord rushed upon him, and although he had nothing in his hand, he tore the lion in pieces as one tears a young goat" (Judges 14:5–6). The lion's carcass became a place of honey for a swarm of bees.

A few days later Samson found himself in a compromising situation with his Philistine in-laws. In an effort to impress them, Samson asked them a difficult riddle: "Out of the eater came something to eat. Out of the strong came something sweet" (Judges 14:14). They were duly stumped. There was no way the Philistines could have figured that one out.

The Philistines became angry. They plotted to kill Samson. Samson thought he was pretty hot stuff. He thought he was too sexy for his shirt. He didn't even see the train headed his way. Not once did Samson even stop to consider God's role and perspective in his life. As far as Samson was concerned, God owed him. After all, he hadn't cut his hair in forever. He'd done his part of the bargain, now God could do the rest.

I hate to admit it, but I know about that kind of thinking. I figure if I pull my share then God ought to pull His too. I remind God of all I've done for Him: I haven't had sex before marriage. I give to church regularly. I read my Bible every day. Heck, I even teach the Bible any chance I get. Surely my prayers ought to be answered. Surely my dreams should come true.

I use God to get what I want. I'm confused when the waiting goes on and I don't see results. I tell myself the lie that I deserve more than I've been given. I believe the lie of self-righteousness.

DEEP DOWN, I knew that it was all about me, even though I'd tried to convince myself that He was the reason for my ambitions.

Have you ever asked yourself why God would allow a trial in your life when you've been nothing but faithful, obedient, and good? Just like Samson, we start believing our own press. Just like Samson, we look at our tresses longingly, impressed with our own ability to grow hair. How silly we are. How self-centered we can be.

3. "I can do even better than this": the tragedy of personal ambition.

I remember the exact moment I read Jeremiah 45:5: "And do you seek great things for yourself? Seek them not." It was only a few months before that day that I'd sensed God calling me to ministry. My goals were now "Christian," so I figured I had free rein to dream big for God. Pretty soon my own personal ambitions took over. I wanted a bigger Sunday school class, more opportunities to speak at retreats, more followers on my blog, and a bigger circle of influence. It didn't matter how good things looked to others, I constantly felt as if I could do even better. I tried to spiritualize it. It was all for God, after all. Couldn't God win more people? Couldn't He expand my platform even more?

But deep down I knew that it was all about me, even

though I'd tried to convince myself that He was the reason for my ambitions. While I'm sure that some of my motives were pure and that I really did want to glorify the Lord, there was still too much Lina in the equation.

For Samson, his main ambition was for more love. This guy was blinded by love. It didn't matter what God had called him to do, Samson had one aim in his mind, and it included just one more beautiful lady at his side. Time and again he opted for his own goals over God's. The result was tragic.

Have your own personal ambitions ever clouded your vision and filled you with pride? Have your own goals and personal accomplishments superseded God's will for your life? Are you so interested in your own desires that you can barely recognize God's voice anymore? Perhaps like Samson, God needs to strip you of your pride.

4. "Don't they know who I am?": the foolishness of fame.

Samson was consumed by a lust for recognition and personal glory. In Judges 15, Samson arrogantly defeated the Philistines in revenge for losing his wife. He cunningly tricked the Philistines into battle and destroyed one thousand men with the jawbone of a donkey. In Judges 15:18, Samson, tired from the battle, felt as if he was dying of thirst. He cried out to God saying: "You have granted this great salvation by the hand of your servant, and shall I now die of thirst and fall into the hands of the uncircumcised?"

On first glance, it looks like a statement of faith, but Samson's heart is far from faithful. In his own self-seeking way, Samson was telling God, "Look at all I've done for You, God. Are You going to let someone as great and mighty as I am just die? Don't You know who I am? Don't You see that I deserve water after destroying Your Philistines? You're lucky to have me, God. Now feed me. Quench me. Meet my need."

It was all about me, me, me.

Have you ever found yourself pursuing your own agenda while trying to serve the Lord? Motives are hard to discern. We tell ourselves we are seeking God's glory and desiring His fame, but we quickly get entangled with our own self in the middle. The best way to tell if your motives are godly is to consider these questions:

- What happens when the thing you desire is taken away?
- What do you do when others criticize you or misunderstand you, then judge you harshly for it?
- Do you get upset and think badly about those who criticize you, or can you still lovingly serve them? What happens when you don't get the praise you think you deserve for the job you did?
- Do you still have joy in the Lord, or do you find yourself upset and short-tempered?
- What happens when you do something amazing for the Lord and no one ever finds out or thanks you for it?

There's only one name that matters: the name and renown of the Lord Jesus Christ. All other names will fade. Only His name remains. Are you living your life obsessed with making His name great, or are you too preoccupied with your own?

Fortunately for Samson, the story did not end with his stubborn, self-centered pride. God had committed Himself

ONE WOMAN. One man. One nap. One haircut.

to Samson, and He would be faithful to accomplish His will in Samson's life at any cost.

For Samson, the cost was high, and the pain deep. One woman. One nap. One haircut. Life would never be the same again for him. When he woke up from his nap, Samson's head felt a little bit lighter. His hair was now gone but so was his strength.

God, in His grace, destroyed every bit of pride from Samson's life. The stripping process was not easy, but it left Samson a changed man, ready to be used by God for the purpose that God had intended for him all along.

HOW GOD STRIPS HIS CHILDREN OF PRIDE

As I consider God's pattern in Scripture, I see three specific ways that God uses to strip His followers of pride.

1. God removes our pride through personal failure.

I am not the first person to learn dependence on the Lord through personal failure nor will I be the last. I wish it wasn't so. In some ways my story is much more benign than Samson's. My hair did not have to be shorn. My eyes were never poked out. I didn't become a slave although it did feel as if I'd lost my freedom.

It was a season in my life that I've tried to forget. First came the broken engagement, then the broken heart. I thought I'd hit rock bottom and that things would start looking up. I was wrong.

It was around that time that God called me into full-time ministry. I thought it was the biggest step of faith I'd ever taken. I thought I understood why God had allowed my heart to be broken. I thought a lot of little reasons to make sense of my life. The only thing I didn't think yet was how little I knew of God and His ways: God was just getting started removing the dross from my life.

Because I was teaching a fruitful Bible study at the time, I assumed that God would continue to grow it and keep me in that city for a while. Because I'd obeyed God and accepted His call to ministry, I assumed that He would honor me by doing awesome God things in my life.

Instead, I soon had to move to a new town where I knew no one and was no one. I had no ministry contacts and felt I'd taken ten steps back in my quest to serve the Lord. Instead of a bustling women's Bible study, I found myself co-teaching an inner-city fourth grade Sunday school class. It felt like I was starting all over again from scratch.

That was also the year that I failed my medical boards. I'd never failed anything before. I was devastated. It was like I'd stepped into one long, dark tunnel with no opening in sight. I was free-falling and lonely.

Just like Samson around the prison mill, I found myself walking blindly around and around with nowhere to go. The ministry life I thought I could handle I now knew I could not. The things I thought I deserved had been painfully ripped out of my life. Outwardly, things looked the same. I kept going to church. I kept reading my Bible. I kept praying. But my life was in crisis. I remained under the trial, waiting for who knows what.

And then one day, I let go. In my brokenness I finally

understood what God had been trying to tell me all along. God had not called me to a job. He had called me to Himself. My inability to measure up was my gateway to greater dependence on the Lord. My own failure was the key to my freedom from self. Absolute surrender was the pathway to joy.

2. God removes our pride through painful loss.

I haven't been to many funerals in my life, but I've certainly felt the agony of loss. The summer before I answered the call to ministry I experienced a deep and stinging loss. God inexplicably removed a very tender and precious relationship from my life. I didn't see then what I clearly see now: that relationship had become more important to me than the Lord. I had come to the place in my life where I felt that God owed me that relationship because of what I'd done to deserve it. I had kept my part of the Christian bargain, I'd even prayed in Jesus' name that God would settle up the details, and now all I had to do was sit back and see God make my life work out according to my ways. I had it all mapped out.

Nothing but pride convinces us that God is waiting to do our bidding for us. We hand Him a list of demands and fully anticipate that He will make it happen, as if the God of the whole universe, the God who created all there is, is waiting to do what we tell Him to do.

When we get to that place, God has to remove those things in our life that become more important to us than He is.

For me, in that season of my life, it was a relationship. For you reading this book today, it could be a ministry or a job or a dream. Has the thing you long for become more important to you than the Lord? It is only by losing something of great value that space is made for the Lord to step in and show you that He is far more valuable and sufficient than the thing that was lost.

Samson lost his hair. He lost his wife. He lost his reputation and his strength and his dignity. But God was just getting started with him. His story wasn't over yet and neither is yours. When God calls you to Himself, nothing will stand in the way of His purposes for your life. He is faithful to you to the end.

3. God removes our pride through public humiliation.

Personal failure and painful loss are bad enough. What could be worse? When God strips you of pride, He often uses one more means to do so: total and utter public humiliation.

Can you picture Samson, now blind, walking around the mill, head hung low, listening to the jeering, the laughter, the mocking of the Philistines?

Do you ever wonder why God allows His children to suffer total and utter humiliation as a means of stripping them of their pride? Consider how allowed Himself go to through total and public humiliation—the King of the universe, blameless and without pride, was made a servant for our sakes. He does not ask us to put on something He Himself did not. The next time you're tempted to question God's goodness in your humiliation, think of the Captain of our salvation and how He suffered for you. Isaiah 53:3 tells us that "he was despised and rejected by men; a man of sorrows and acquainted with grief; and as one from whom men hide their faces he was despised, and we esteemed him not."

For me the most brutal form of public humiliation

came through a physical disfigurement that I loathed: I was plagued with adult acne in my late twenties, ironically coinciding with my answering the call to full-time ministry. In a world where beauty is idolized and appearances are emphasized, I felt as if this was a disfigurement I couldn't hide, no matter how hard I tried. It felt as if it was an outward sign of failure that I couldn't ignore. It was a problem I had a hard time eradicating.

Over the years, much of my pride has been rooted in my appearance and performance. When pride gets caught in a performance cycle, it can only be destroyed through public humiliation.

Though I could hide most hurts and failures in my life, there was no way I could hide my face. Each time I stood in front of a crowd to teach, I wondered what they saw. Each time I stood in front of a crowd to teach, I was forced to rest fully on the Lord to work through me despite me. Just like Samson, I walked round and round the mill, head hung low, waiting for my hair to grow out.

THOUGH I COULD hide most hurts and failures in my life, there was no way I could hide my face.

One day it finally did.

FINALLY SOME GOOD NEWS

We do not serve a God who takes great joy in torturing us. God is not a fickle God who looks down on His children and sees how far He can push us. God's stripping process is loving and gentle and purposeful, and it ends at the exact time that He knows is best.

And soon, just like Samson, my heart grew soft and my eyes saw light. One day, Samson looked up to the Lord and said what God was longing to hear all along:

"O Lord God . . ." (Judges 16:28).

It had been years since Samson had uttered those words of dependence. It had been years since Samson had looked upward.

My Lord. My God. To the One who made me the promise, to the only One who can. God, you were right all along. Your ways are in fact higher than my ways. Your plans are better than my plans.

"O Lord God."
Have Your way in me, no matter what. Have Your way in me, come what may. I choose You over my desires. I choose You over my own ambitions. I choose You over my pride. I choose You.

In Isaiah 28:27–29 we're told that "dill is not threshed with a threshing sledge, nor is a cart wheel rolled over cumin, but dill is beaten out with a stick, and cumin with a rod."

Samson had been stripped, beaten, and rolled over, but he was finally ready to be used by God. In a moment of complete dependence on the Lord, Samson's strength came back one last time, and he was able to live out the purpose God had for him all along. It's told that more Philistines died on the day of Samson's death than those whom he had killed during his entire lifetime.

Is God stripping you of your pride? Are you still trying to accomplish His plans your ways? Perhaps it's time to learn a few lessons from stupid Samson. Or maybe he wasn't really stupid after all. Maybe he was just broken in exactly the right places.

More importantly, maybe God was mending him in exactly the right places.

Though you may not see it right now, He's doing the same for you. He doesn't need you to be too sexy for your shirt. All He wants from you is your total and complete dependence on Him.

Three years ago we decided to make a huge change in our lives when my husband accepted a position with a different company. While his pay was going to be cut in half, we were sure that it was the right choice because it would allow him to be home more and have a better family/work balance. We boldly stated that we were trusting God on all fronts. The move took us far from family and friends, but we believed we had each other.

I wasn't prepared for the hardships we would face. In taking the new job, my husband lost his support system. I felt very alone. I felt drained of all hope. I was living in strange place where I didn't know anyone. My kids were missing their friends and family terribly and didn't understand why they never saw Daddy. My husband was exhausted, emotionally and physically.

I began to question whether it had really been God calling us to change jobs and move. Gradually, God did restore us and made it clear that it was His calling for us to move. He did sustain. He did provide for our need. The best part is that His church became our home, our family, and our place of work. While I will never fully understand the waiting, I do know it was well worth it.

—Becky

Chapter Four

PERFECTLY LONELY

*Bare heights of loneliness . . . a wilderness whose
burning winds sweep over glowing sands, what are they
to Him? Even there He can refresh us, even there He can
renew us.* —Amy Carmichael

I've always been well-liked, even in my junior high, extremely
nerdy days. I grew up in a home that strongly supported me
and made me feel like I could shoot for the moon. Teachers
loved my quick wit and good grades. Friends laughed at my
jokes and applauded my antics.

The problem with being well-liked is that you soon turn
into a person who can't function without being well-liked.

Let me explain.

Everything went according to plan until my late twenties when I began missing some major milestones in my life.
Instead of getting married like everyone else did, I got in the
habit of breaking off engagements. Instead of having kids, I
got degrees. Instead of blossoming into my beautiful adult
facial structure, I got acne that wouldn't go away. And instead
of learning to love and appreciate people, I began to either depend on them for my happiness, or avoid them in my shame.

My own personal people crisis couldn't have come at a
worse time. I had felt a calling in my late twenties to teach
the Bible to women. Around that time I started joking that
ministry would be great were it not for the people.

It wasn't funny.

I had a people problem, and God was going to strip me of it. People are difficult to handle on a good day. They want too much from you and they aren't ashamed to ask for it. Despite that, it doesn't take long for us to realize we can't live without them.

And for better or for worse, God's plans for us include people, with all of their idiosyncrasies and nuances.

He promised Abraham not one child but many, many kids. He had Moses lead thousands upon thousands of people out of Egypt. He put David in charge of lots and lots of people. He Himself came to save the entire world. His legacy to us, His followers, is the church that He compared to a body and described as a group of broken but redeemed men and women through whom He would show His love and grace to others.

God loves people more than anything, and He will do whatever it takes to help us keep people in proper perspective in our lives. His desire is to free us from needing people and bring us to the place where we can love them freely instead. He longs for us to stop fearing people and start serving them instead.

FOUR WAYS TO MISMANAGE PEOPLE

The problem is that we have a tendency to mismanage people. There are four primary ways we tend to do this.

1. We idolize them.

When I was eight years old I had to have abdominal surgery. Shortly after the operation, while I was still in the hospital, the wound got infected. One sunny morning while my grandmother sat beside me, the surgeon came by to check me. He noticed that the wound had some pus draining from its edges. Before I had time to blink, the surgeon had taken a knife and begun debriding the wound right there at the bedside. Debriding, in case you're wondering, is when you remove dead or infected layers of skin to clean up a wound. It's not pretty, but it must be done for healing to take place. I'm sure you could hear me scream all the way down in the hospital cafeteria. I'd never experienced anything so painful in my life.

Over the years I have had a tendency to idolize certain people in my life. I did it for ten years with a man I thought

I HAD A people problem.

was my soul mate. He became my source of security and the person I turned to for comfort. I have done it repeatedly with people I have looked up to in ministry. Instead of trusting the Lord to open the way for me, I have leaned on other people to do it. Each and every time I have been tempted to idolize people, God has seen my infected soul and put His scalpel to work, ridding me of the unnecessary pus.

As painful as debriding an infection is, the surgeon does it because he is far more concerned with the long-term health of his patients than he is with their comfort. God is the most skillful surgeon there is. He sees our strongholds and gently but painfully strips us of the things that we idolize. He does it for our own good.

You may be reading this and wondering what kind of God would do something like that to His children. The answer is simple. Only a God who knows that true satisfaction can be met in Him alone would allow such pain to His children. Only a God who longs for our joy would be willing to bring such suffering to His own. He's the same God who led His Son to the cross. He's a God of love and a God who longs to meet you in your deepest longings.

I know this because He's done it for me. As long as people occupy a big portion of our heart, there is no room for God in it. It is in the ensuing emptiness that we can finally open the door to our heart and let the Lord in.

We are living in a time of Christian celebrities. It's easy to get obsessed with "famous" Christians and rely on them for our answers. The moment our favorite "celebrities" fail us, as they most surely will, we sense our growing resentment and become more cynical about the life of faith. There is no room for idolizing people while serving the living God. You can be sure that God will do whatever it takes to guard our hearts for worshiping Him alone.

2. We fear them.

There is a very powerful verse in Proverbs 29:25: "The fear of man lays a snare, but whoever trusts in the Lord is safe." A snare is meant to kill you. Sadly, so does a pattern of living in the fear of man. Unfortunately most of us know that feeling too well and have fallen prey to it all too often.

Peter understood the fear of man well. He left his fishing nets in response to Christ's call. He walked closely with Jesus for three years, yet on the evening of Christ's crucifixion Peter couldn't even stand up to a servant girl. Before the cock crowed, Peter denied Jesus Christ three times. God was in the process of stripping Peter of his pride and his dependence on others.

In the early days of my blog, I spent countless hours worrying about how many followers I had, how fast my subscribers were growing, and my Google analytics. I felt a constant pressure to blog the right thing. While I knew that God was sovereign over my life in the general sense, and while I verbally acknowledged that my motives were pure, the truth revealed that my heart was captured by the fear of man and the desire to please others.

Nothing will steal your joy like a life that is dedicated to pleasing people. Nothing will break God's heart more than your persistence to appease others. God never intended for us to live like that. He is committed to stripping us of our fear of man at any cost.

3. We envy them.

I am a very competitive person. I suppose you can't get into medical school without some level of competitiveness. But my true colors didn't become glaring until well into my call to ministry. All of a sudden I didn't feel good enough, and I had numerous ways to confirm it including Twitter, Facebook, blogs, Pinterest, Instagram, and many others.

I developed a list of "Christian women leaders" that I followed on these social networking sites. The better they seemed to do, the worse I felt. Why did they have more followers than I did? Why did their blogs seem to grow so fast while mine slowly eked by? I felt neglected by God and on the outskirts of some imaginary huddle that I contrived and nothing could convince me otherwise.

You may not think you've been plagued with the green-eyed monster, but it's an infection that's easier to acquire than you think, especially in our generation. Jealousy is an age-old struggle, and it is a huge deal. We tend to underrate it or minimize its severity, but listen to Romans 13:13–14:

> Let us walk properly as in the daytime, not in orgies and drunkenness, not in sexual immorality and sensuality, not in quarreling and jealousy. But put on the Lord Jesus Christ, and make no provision for the flesh, to gratify its desires.

It's mind blowing, isn't it? God puts envy and jealousy on the same list with sexual orgies and immorality! Is it any surprise that God is committed to stripping His followers of people-pleasing in His desire to see us walk more freely?

4. We seek their approval.

If I have one favorite love language, it's this: words of affirmation. I love to be patted on the back and recognized. One of the ways I have mismanaged people is by looking to them for approval and grow my already-inflated ego.

One of the ways God has had to strip me of my pride is by stripping me of the people who I have looked to for approval. At the risk of sounding pathetic, I'm going to tell you more about it.

Over the last few years, for a variety of reasons, I've had some amazing chances to meet some wonderful and—may I add—famous Christians. It shouldn't be a big deal but in our Western, Hollywood mindset, it is. A normal person would simply be thankful and thrilled for the opportunity to meet any number of wonderful Christian teachers, but I'm not your average normal person. I am a people-pleaser. I am an approval-seeker.

So instead, I've turned into a stalker.

I tweet these famous friends. I email them when I can. I play Words with Friends with them. And when they ignore me, as most people should ignore a stalker, my feelings get hurt. "God," I wonder out loud, "why are Your other children so mean to me? Why do You always want me to feel like I'm on the outside looking in? Do You love Your other kids more than You love me? Don't You even like me?"

PLEASING MAN and pleasing God are mutually exclusive. You cannot do both.

Pretty soon my own ignorant behavior turns into an accusation of God's goodness and His character (I warned you it was pathetic, didn't I?).

Paul asked a formidable question in Galatians 1:10: "For am I now seeking the approval of man, or of God?" There is no room for people-pleasing in the life of the one who has answered Christ's call. God will go to great extent to uproot this sin from the heart of His followers. In an effort to strip me of the desire to please others, God has allowed me to endure some pretty strong rejections that have ultimately been for my good.

If you have a tendency to look to others for approval in your life, God will do whatever it takes to strip you of this lie. He longs to show you that you can rest in the truth that He has already accepted you in Christ.

Pleasing man and pleasing God are mutually exclusive. You cannot do both. Which are you choosing?

THE SECRET OF THE WILDERNESS

If you've responded to God's call in your life, chances are you're either in the wilderness, are headed to the wilderness, or have just come out of the of wilderness. Throughout the pages of Scripture you will find that the most popular place to learn God's ways is smack in the middle of the wilderness. Every single person who has been greatly used by God has had to go through the wilderness.

Take David for example. Shortly after he's anointed by Samuel to be the king of Israel, he miraculously kills Goliath. Everybody loves David for a while. He's young and handsome and he's on a winning streak that is sure to get him the Heisman. Even King Saul becomes enamored with David.

It didn't take long for the tide to turn for David, as the next ten years would show. David spent those years running away from Saul, hiding in a cave of the greatest wilderness of his life. How could a guy who was so obviously called by God end up hiding for his life? For a while, David was as alone as one could get.

It is out of this loneliness that emerged one of the strongest kings of all times. David would become known as a man after God's own heart. He emerged as a man committed to the Lord and strong in His might. David's time in the wilderness yielded a man now free to rule a nation. The lesson is obvious: when there's no one around to impress, the Lord will impress your heart with His presence.

David is not the only follower of God who found himself

in the wilderness. All the way from Abraham, to Moses, to the great prophet Elijah, the wilderness is a familiar place for the one who God has called. The New Testament is also filled with examples of Christ's followers who learned to be alone with the Lord. There's Paul, who went to the desert alone for three years before God launched him into ministry. Peter often found himself alone on a rooftop or in a prison cell. And John, the beloved disciple, wrote some of his best books exiled on an island.

It is when surrounded by the deafening silence that the soul quiets enough to hear God speak. It is when others become shadows allowing God's presence to settle over you that you will finally understand that without Christ you can do nothing, be nothing, and accomplish nothing.

Do you know the wilderness of loneliness? Are you in it now?

I am quite familiar with being alone. I have lived alone for over twenty years now. To be honest with you, I like it that way. It's peaceful and allows me the freedom to write. But the wilderness of loneliness that I'm referring to is not one you seek by choice. I'm talking about a wilderness that can hit you in the midst of a crowded room or when you're wide awake at three in the morning. You suddenly feel an ache that you don't quite recognize. You long for something, for someone.

You almost feel afraid.

My initial instinct is to misunderstand that kind of loneliness. I resent it. I hate it. I long to escape it. I am tempted to check my email or Facebook. I turn on the television and strain for the noise of human voices. I yearn to fill the noise in the gaping hole of my heart.

It catches me by surprise, this aching loneliness. It's like an uninvited guest that I can't quite bid farewell; it hovers over me. I close my eyes in the hope that sleep will erase it, but I wake up and it's still there. I find it my constant companion.

Are you familiar with this kind of wilderness? It may be a wilderness that comes from the rejection of those by whom you long to be accepted. It may be a wilderness that comes from seeing people as they really are, sinners in need of grace. It may even be a wilderness that comes from being forgotten by others.

It is precisely in this wilderness that God waits to step in and fill your deepest longings. Can you hear in your wilderness the loving voice of One calling out your name?

Few verses have ministered to me like the words of the prophet Hosea in Hosea 2:14–15: "Therefore, behold, I will allure her, and bring her into the wilderness, and speak tenderly to her. And there I will give her her vineyards and make the Valley of Achor a door of hope."

God tenderly calls out to you in the wilderness. The problem is that most of us are not trained to hear His voice. Even worse, most of us resist hearing His voice, longing for something else to fill us. We have replaced the knowledge of God with the worship of people.

HOW TO RIGHTLY RELATE TO PEOPLE

If you're tracking with me on this topic, you may be tempted to admit: "Okay, I give. I won't speak to another human being as long as I live."

And you'd completely miss the point. God's heart is for

people. His goal is not to put us in a place of ascetic isolation where only He has access to our lives. In fact, in Proverbs 18:1 God says: "Whoever isolates himself seeks his own desire; he breaks out against all sound judgment."

GOD'S GOAL IN stripping us of people is not to isolate us but to teach us to rightly relate to others.

Trust me, there are days I long to isolate myself from others. There are days when listening to one more sob story threatens to undo me, and I feel suffocated by the presence of people in my life.

God loves people. When He chose to show us His extreme love, He took on the form of a man and lived among us. It was His desire to be with us. He chose us. On those rare occasions when He tried to get away from people and still found himself surrounded by a crowd, He didn't resent them. On the contrary, the Bible continually speaks of Jesus seeing large crowds and having compassion on them.

God's goal in stripping us of people is not to isolate us but to teach us to rightly relate to others. When He becomes all we need, we are finally free to rightly relate to other people out of the overflow of His presence in us.

I'd like to give you three ways that God would have us rightly relate to people.

1. God wants us to love people.

This one is a no-brainer. God is love. That a God of love would want us to love others seems so obvious, but how easily we miss it. Instead of loving others, we look to be loved by them. Instead of pouring ourselves into them, we push them to pour into us.

Maybe you think you love others. The best test of your love for others takes place when people don't do what you want them to do. Do you get angry with them? Do you try to manipulate them to do what you want? Do you hold grudges against others because they didn't say what you want them to say?

The kind of love that God longs for us to display to others is the kind of love that Jesus has shown us. It is a love that is patient and long-suffering. It is a love that is kind and gentle. It does not envy or boast. It is not arrogant or rude. It does not insist on its own way. It is not irritable or resentful. It does not rejoice in wrongdoing, but it rejoices in the truth. It is a love that bears all things, believes all things, hopes all things, and endures all things. It never ends.

It's the kind of love that slowly walked up a hill with a cross piercing His back, willingly and wrongfully hanging on a tree until death finally took over. It is a love that seems senseless in the moment but later reveals itself to be the turning point for life.

It is the kind of love that reached down and pulled me out of a pit so deep, when no one else would even look at me because of the filth that surrounded me. It is a love that sits with me when I can't see through my own tears of self-pity and gently reminds me that I am loved and am not forgotten.

It is a love that has patiently waited for me while layer after layer of my stripped skin finally healed. It is a love that fills me to overflowing and longs for me to reach out and touch others with its healing balm.

I don't deserve this love. I don't deserve this Jesus. But He's mine because of His great love.

2. God wants us to serve people.

We can talk about love until we're blue in the face, but you know what they say about words: they're cheap. They're useless if you don't put your money where your mouth is. If you're studying the language of love, service is the currency that Christ used to demonstrate His perfect love for others.

Do you long to be served or, like Christ, do you seek to serve others? It's easy to serve those you love, respect, and look up to. It's a lot harder to serve the ones who can't pay you back. It's a lot harder to serve the ones who insult you and don't ever thank you.

Jesus exemplified perfect servanthood when on the eve of His crucifixion He bent down, took a towel, and washed His disciples' feet. They didn't understand it. They almost resented it and tried to fight it. They offered to do the washing instead. But Christ was adamant: "He who is least among you all is the one who is great" (Luke 9:48). The King had made Himself a servant to demonstrate for us exactly what it meant to love others. He knew what it meant to be counted as nothing. He knew what it meant to give up every sense of personal right as need after need was met with love.

There is no love like Christ's love. Do you know this kind of love? Have you been radically changed by Christ's love? Only your selfless service for others can adequately tell how well you understand Christ's perfect love.

3. God wants us to enjoy people.

It's easy to become leery of people and develop an attitude that is weighed down by the demands of people, living with a constant sense of martyrdom for all you do to serve others.

Throughout the gospels, Christ was never confused for a martyr. Not once do we feel sorry for Him. Though He spent all of His life giving to others, healing others, pouring Himself into others, He never once seemed to lack in love. He was so confident of His Father's love that He was able to live with a strong sense of preordained purpose and a willingness to yield Himself fully to God's purposes.

Jesus Christ enjoyed people. He loved the disciples. He was a friend of sinners. His first miracle was at a wedding. His last activity before dying was a dinner with His friends. And He continues to take great joy in us today.

It is only as God frees us from the demands of people and teaches us to rightly relate to them that we can truly enjoy them as He did. It is when we understand His deep love for us that we can be free of the sense of expectation that other people place on us and live in the sphere of influence He has intended for us.

The great prophet Elijah found himself in a great wilderness once. It came at a surprising time in his life, immediately following a great victory. No matter the reasons, he felt utterly and absolutely alone. From Elijah's perspective, the entire world had forgotten him while he tirelessly toiled away for the Lord. Nobody cared about him, nobody saw his aching loneliness, not even God.

It was in the pitch black of a lonely cave that Elijah was

finally quiet enough to hear God's voice.

It's a funny thing about God. He knows we're too stubborn to come to Him when we're in trouble, so He comes to us instead. He knows we're not wise enough to understand what He's up to, so He reaches down to us and explains.

"What are you doing here?" He asked.

And then the amazing happens. Instead of finding God in the big things, instead of seeing God in the crowd, Elijah got it. In the quiet of the cave, in the darkness of his loneliness, in the stillness of the day, Elijah was finally able to hear God's whisper.

You can best hear God in the stillness. You can best hear God in the quiet. You can best know the Father when you're perfectly lonely.

And when you're alone enough to listen, you'll hear Him whisper: *You are loved. You are dear. You are seen. Your future is secure. You are known. And you are never alone.*

And that's more than enough for today.

I tend to learn lessons the hard way. God has to literally pry open my white-knuckled fingers to get me to release areas of my life over to Him. Four years ago, I attended an event where they asked us to write down what we treasured and hand it over to the Lord by putting it in a container. God had been revealing to me that perfectionism was what I treasured most in life. Little did I know that only a few days after submitting that slip of paper, I would become extremely ill and be put into a position where everything became out of my control. My perfect little world came crashing down on me.

My health was stripped away, my control of my home was stripped away, my strength was stripped away, even my well-planned future was stripped away from me as I waited to see what recovery and healing would be like. It took years for me to recover. It was one of the most difficult periods in my life and yet one of the best things that has ever happened to me. I can't believe how many ways God has used that dark part of my life, and I might never fully understand the depth of what He did. I am thankful.

—Liz

Chapter Five

WE'RE NOT IN KANSAS ANYMORE

He is no fool who gives what he cannot keep to gain what he cannot lose. —Jim Elliot

It was a hot, dark night—dark enough that I couldn't see my hand in front of my face or the mosquito net threatening to suffocate my head. The flapping of bats' wings hovered too near, the smell of the makeshift toilet (a bucket by my hammock) too close for comfort.

I was in the middle of nowhere in the Venezuelan Amazon rain forest. It had taken four planes and a long walk to finally make it to this hut, and along with two other American women and the missionary guide, our medical missions team was tucked in for the night. The Indian tribe we were visiting had never laid eyes on a Western woman before. It's a lot of pressure trying to represent the free world under these circumstances. We were here to bring both medical supplies and the gospel of Jesus Christ—promising healing to both bodies and souls; yet all I could think about was how long I could hold it without having to use the bucket toilet on my right. Would I last the three days until the Cessna that dropped us off would finally reappear on the horizon? All bets were on.

No one warned me it would be so hard. No one mentioned how uncomfortable God's call would be. As I waited for the sun to creep up, I understood what the rest of the team had already figured out: Kansas wasn't even in our rearview mirrors anymore.

We in the Western world tend to be creatures of comfort. I suppose everyone everywhere wants comfort, but it's a lot more obvious in the land of the free where a Big Mac can be purchased any time of the day or night without even having to get out of your car. If you think of it—whatever "it" may be—it can be yours with a single tap of your finger. Overnight mail is an insult to immediate delivery.

CONSIDER THE LAST time you went without electricity for longer than a week.

Is it any wonder that most of us approach God's call with the same expectations, the same demands, and the same cravings for personal comfort that we have come to expect in our daily lives? The concept of waiting, or ever going without, seems too foreign and too third world for us. We have become far more civilized, far more advanced, and far too spoiled for old-fashioned, biblical methods.

The words of Jesus Christ in the New Testament enthrall us, suspend us, but seem an echo of days gone by. We may be willing to give up some of our stuff, so long as we get the newest model to replace what's now gone. But to give up our dreams? We come to Jesus with faith, the same Jesus who can do anything, and expect He will accommodate our plans (or *else*). We're doing it all for Him, after all, aren't we?

Do I sound too harsh? Forgive me. I don't mean to offend your sensibilities, but consider the last time you went without electricity for longer than a week. Or think about the last time you had to wait in line for a loaf of bread.

I know I sound like your father whining about walking three miles uphill to school both ways, but the truth is that we are living in dangerous times of comfort. We are facing a new culture of ease that is not compatible with New Testament Christianity where sacrifice and simplicity rule the day.

I'm not advocating poverty or simplicity for the sake of some self-sacrificing joyride (God knows I love my iPhone way too much for that), but in this chapter we're going to discuss the next step in the stripping process. I'm going to show you how God will strip His children of the security blankets and comfort measures that threaten to lull us into a spiritual coma.

It's time to wake up, Christian. Open your eyes and you'll see: the bats are closer than you think. It's time to focus on what matters the most. It's time to live like we believe the gospel: heaven is our home. This earth is passing by. People need the Lord. Life is shorter than you think.

The missionary guide gave us just one rule as we boarded the Cessna that would drop us into the Amazon village on that hot, dark night: "You must leave behind anything that will weigh you down," he said. There was no room for toys and gadgets and distractions. Only the basics were permitted. Our journey to the jungle took on a wartime mentality.

We as Christians have forgotten that we must maintain a wartime mentality. Christ did not save us to give us heaven here on earth. We are on a journey home, where we will one day have peace and joy and rest. But for now, we must lift up our arms and fight. We must let go of the things that weigh us down and run with endurance the race set before us. Many things stand in our way, but God in His grace will do what He can to free us from them.

A PARABLE TO CONSIDER

Jesus tells a great parable in Luke 14:16–24. A man gave a great banquet and invited many. As the invitations went out, excuses came in. "I can't come, I just bought some land," one said. "I can't come, I just bought an ox," said another. "I can't come, I just got married" . . . the excuses went on and on. The master became angry and sent his servant back out to invite the ones who would come: the blind, the lame, the poor, the crippled.

Jesus concluded the parable with a great assertion in verse 33: "So therefore, any one of you who does not renounce all that he has cannot be my disciple."

"Does not renounce all that he has." That sounds a bit intense to me. It sounds almost radical to me. It sounds life changing and demanding. Give up your nets. Follow me. It seemed easy at first. But somewhere between dropping my nets and giving up my iPhone, God's call to follow Him took on a drastic turn.

The smell of the bucket toilet is excruciating. The noise of the bats is too near. In the darkness of the night, I feel like bailing; I dream of being pulled out of the jungle in a Bond-like chopper. In the quiet of the midnight hour, I long for the comforts of home and the ease of a life void of sacrifice.

Do you struggle in the same way that I do? Do you long for a life that is unencumbered with stuff and is ready to go wherever the Lord leads? I'd like you to consider four areas

God wants to strip from the lives of His followers.

FOUR COMFORTS THAT MUST GO

There is a cost to following Jesus. I'm not talking about just money. I'm not talking about just stuff. I'm talking about everything. God became a man and died on the cross for us. He gave us His all. He demands our all in return. His call is not a multiple-choice menu where we can select the options we like for our own version of Christianity. His call is an all or nothing, black or white, all-in or all-out call.

I'd like to point out four misconceptions about comforts that threaten to hinder us from following God's call:

1. Material possessions as the highest good.

Let me start by saying this: God doesn't need your money. He's not asking you to give up your BMW or move into a shack. If He needs something, He's got it covered. He owns the cattle on a thousand hills. He made the world and everything in it. When His disciples needed a few bucks for taxes, He gave them a fish that spewed out the cash. He can do anything, and He doesn't need anything.

We, on the other hand, are temporal creatures and quickly forget that God is the One who gave us all that we have. It doesn't take long for us to stop relying on the Lord and to become completely reliant on the stuff He has given us. Another way to say it is that it's not important how much stuff we have, but the important thing is: Does it have us?

I grew up in the seventies in Lebanon. It was a time of war. We often went for weeks without electricity. We didn't have television or computers. There were days we didn't have water, and we often had to stock up on bread and other items to make sure we had enough to eat. (I am sure you're impressed . . . can you believe I'm still alive to tell about it?)

What I learned from those days is that the things we think we can't live without, we can. But like so often in life, my memory can become spotty and I quickly forget. Instead of relying on the One who gives me good gifts, I find myself turning to the gifts instead. They become very important to me. The more gifts God gives me, the more I believe that He loves me. And if He ever withholds gifts from me, I start to question His love for me and doubt His goodness in my life.

Instead of worshiping God as the Lord, we have turned Him into a puppet or a type of Santa Claus that we can manipulate at our own whim and for our own uses. If your plan is to use God in order to acquire more stuff in your life, you're in trouble. You may have convinced yourself that your "stuff" doesn't matter to you as much as God does, but the only way to know that for sure is to watch your reactions when you lose some of that stuff.

THE THINGS WE think we can't live without, we can.

Is your stuff getting in the way of your calling? Are you so preoccupied with paying your bills and living a good life here on this earth that your time and attention for heavenly matters have dwindled?

2. Personal relationships as the tie that binds.

I've always liked the gospel of Luke—maybe because it's written by a doctor or maybe because he gave up so much for the ministry or maybe because it's just a great gospel. Let's read Luke 9:57–62 and notice a pattern emerging:

> As they were going along the road, someone said to him, "I will follow you wherever you go." And Jesus said to him, "Foxes have holes, and birds of the air have nests, but the Son of Man has nowhere to lay his head." To another he said, "Follow me." But he said, "Lord, let me first go and bury my father." And Jesus said to him, "Leave the dead to bury their own dead. But as for you, go and proclaim the kingdom of God." Yet another said, "I will follow you, Lord, but let me first say farewell to those at my home." Jesus said to him, "No one who puts his hand to the plow and looks back is fit for the kingdom of God."

According to this passage, one of the key elements holding Christians back from running full-throttle after the Lord is the binding nature of intimate relationships. Libraries are full of stories of missionaries who set sail for unknown lands, leaving disapproving parents behind. It's no wonder Jesus also said in Luke 14:26: "If anyone comes to me and does not hate his own father and mother and wife and children and brothers and sisters, yes, and even his own life, he cannot be my disciple."

Do Christ's words shock you? Were you confused by the call of Jesus Christ? Did you think it would be easy? No wonder we're told that only a few will actually go through the narrow gate.

Relationships are complicated. My friendships are fewer as I get older, but they are better, deeper, and holier. I have found the best measure of a godly friend is one who is willing to speak God's truth in my life instead of telling me what I want to hear. Another measure of a godly friend is one who will stand aside and allow me to follow after what God's call is in my life rather than hold me back in a place of safety and comfort.

What kinds of relationships do you surround yourself with? Do your relationships draw you closer to the Lord Jesus Christ or do they burden you with duties that take you away from serving the Lord? Are you bogged down by the expectations of family or are you daily focusing on what the Lord wants for you that day?

If you're in a season of difficulty when it comes to personal relationships, perhaps God is stripping you of the comfort of relationships in order to make room for what He knows is best.

3. Safety of home as the greatest comfort.

Anyone who has traveled overseas knows of that perfect moment when the plane lands on homeland turf and you're minutes away from a good old-fashioned burger. Everything smells better at home. Everything tastes better at home. We love the idea of home.

Yet over and over again, God's Word reminds us that this earth is not our home. It's not time to settle yet. Paul tells us that our citizenship is in heaven (Philippians 3:20), and the writer of Hebrews 11 drives the same point home in verses 13–14, and 16:

These all died in faith, not having received the things promised, but having seen them and greeted them from afar, and having acknowledged that they were strangers and exiles on the earth. For people who speak thus make it clear that they are seeking a homeland. . . . But as it is, they desire a better country, that is, a heavenly one.

Hebrews 11:24–26 goes on to point to Moses as an example of a man with that same mindset:

By faith Moses, when he was grown up, refused to be called the son of Pharaoh's daughter, choosing rather to be mistreated with the people of God than to enjoy the fleeting pleasures of sin. He considered the reproach of Christ greater wealth than the treasures of Egypt, for he was looking to the reward.

Who would have thought that a man who grew up in the comforts of Pharaoh's home would be willing to give up the lush life of the palace for God's call? But Moses did. He had found Someone greater than all the rewards and treasures of Egypt.

David Livingstone was a missionary doctor in Africa and, in my opinion, one of the greatest Christians who ever lived. He understood Moses's choice. Listen to what he once said:

People talk of the sacrifice I have made in spending so much of my life in Africa. Can that be called a sacrifice which is simply acknowledging a great debt we owe to our God, which we can never repay? Is that a sacrifice which brings its own reward in healthful activity, the consciousness of doing good, peace of mind, and a bright hope of a glorious destiny? It is emphatically no sacrifice. Rather it is a privilege. Anxiety, sickness, suffering, danger, foregoing the common conveniences of this life–these may make us pause, and cause the spirit to waver, and the soul to sink; but let this only be for a moment. All these are nothing compared with the glory which shall later be revealed in and through us. I never made a sacrifice. Of this we ought not to talk, when we remember the great sacrifice which He made who left His Father's throne on high to give Himself for us.[3]

The choice to leave the comforts of home without looking back can only be understood in light of the knowledge of what we have in Christ. He has so much more in store for us who have answered His call, refusing to turn back.

4. Personal abilities as your default measure.

There is a fourth comfort that must be stripped from our lives as we get closer to the heart of the Lord. It is the comfort of our own personal abilities.

There is great comfort in a growing ability to do things. Early on in my medical practice, I knew a lot less but I prayed a whole lot more before each shift. The more I find myself improving as a doctor, the less I find myself turning to the Lord. Once in a while, I see a difficult case that baffles my mind and reminds me that life and healing are in God's hands. I am driven to my knees in these moments.

Confidence and experience are wonderful until you find

yourself defaulting to your own personal abilities as your comfort measure and place of security, instead of turning to the Lord for help.

GOD DOESN'T need our abilities as much as He needs our surrendered hearts.

Soon after I sensed God calling me into full-time ministry, I sat down and considered where my abilities lie. I had done well on the writing segments of every standardized test I'd ever taken, so I figured I'd start a newsletter. That was way back in the nineties when blogs weren't around yet.

People read my newsletters, so I kept writing. Eventually, I transitioned to a blog. At first, only a few people read it. I kept writing. The more people read it, the higher my expectations. I wanted more readers, so I worked harder. I blogged more often. I read a lot about writing. I thought that if I could provide better content, I'd automatically see faster growth. I did a lot of giveaways. I prayed more.

But things didn't change as fast as I wanted them to.

The harder I worked and the more I expected, the more resentment I felt toward God for not making things happen. I had to face a painful reality: Either I really wasn't good enough, or else God was stripping me of my reliance on my own abilities.

Do you remember Peter, the fisherman turned disciple who couldn't even stand up to the servant girl the night of the crucifixion? No one would have confused Peter with a bold preacher of God's Word on the night the cock crowed.

But watch Peter in Acts 2, and you'll see a man who preached a sermon that would change the world. Three thousand people gave their life to Christ on that day.

Now tell me how relevant personal ability is when lined up with God's plan for His children? God doesn't need our abilities as much as He needs our surrendered hearts. After all, He hasn't called us to a job but to Himself. He knows what we are still learning: our greatest comfort is when we are resting only in His will.

BUT, WHY?

Are you starting to wonder why? Why does God systematically remove those things we count dear? Why can't we have it all? Why does it have to be so painful?

The answer becomes clear the moment you surrender to His heart. The answer becomes obvious the moment you yield to Him.

God does it because He knows what is best. He does it because He knows that He is enough.

He sees when I get in the place where things become more important to me than He is. He sees my heart when I long to use Him to get what I want. He sees when I judge Him by what I have instead of by the truth of who He is. He sees when my priorities and my main pursuit deviate from what is best to pursue what feels best at that moment.

And because of His grace, He doesn't allow me to stay in that place.

It is only when I get in the place where I have nothing left—people seem far, possessions don't satisfy, and my own abilities seem irrelevant. It is when I get in the place where I'm at my wits' end that I'm finally ready to acknowledge what God has known all along.

He is all I need.

It is in my moments of weakness that I become completely and desperately dependent on God. It is in those moments of weakness that I'm finally ready to draw near to the heart of God. I stop striving. I stop trying. I stop talking. I stop planning. I stop fretting. I simply stop.

And I am finally ready to open my eyes and see.

THE HEALING AFTER THE HURT

I've noticed something in taking care of kids in the emergency room. When they hurt, they shut their eyes. When they're afraid, they close their eyes really tight. Eventually, by the time the pain medication kicks in and the pain becomes bearable, they tentatively steal a quick peek. Then slowly they keep opening their eyes until they can finally breathe normally again. That's when the fun usually begins. We talk, we laugh. They tell me stories and watch TV and all the while, I do my thing. I sew them up and fix their wounds. I do the healing while we enjoy getting to know one another.

Our journey with the Lord is much like that. At first, the pain seems too much to bear, the losses too drastic to imagine. We close our eyes and fight. Eventually, we stop long enough to steal a peek, and notice that the pain is not meant to hurt us, but to fix us. The more we look and try to see what's happening, the more we realize that we can let go and enjoy the ride. We're not only going to make it, but we're getting better in the process.

What joy there is when we finally see that God is our Great Physician, healing us, helping us, and loving us. He's given us everything we need to live for Him. Instead of the human comforts we think will give us joy, He provides comforts that can never be stolen from us. There are three ways God gives his children comfort.

1. The comfort of His presence.

God's presence brings peace. His presence brings comfort. Nothing in this world can threaten to steal His presence from your life. Nothing can separate you from His love. He's just a prayer away. The old hymn says, "O what peace we often forfeit, O what needless pain we bear, all because we do not carry everything to God in prayer."[4] The Holy Spirit Himself is described as our comforter on several occasions in the New Testament (John 15:26). He is ours to stay.

Do you need a reminder of God's presence today? He is nearer than your nearest friend. He is near even when you do not feel His presence. He is near you when you doubt Him. He is all the comfort you need.

2. The safety of His promises.

The surest way to know God's nearness is to hold on to His promises. He has given us so many promises in His Word. Many of His followers have experienced great victories by hanging on to God's promises for life.

When I was young, I was taught to claim God's promises, especially when making big decisions. I have found this practice lifesaving. The pattern in the Christian life is that when you take any step of faith, instead of seeing immediate relief, you will typically first face some time of testing. It used to surprise me when that happened, but not anymore.

Now I just hang on to God's promises during those times of waiting and testing.

God may have stripped me of the comforts of people and possessions and abilities, but He has given me a chest full of the treasures of His promises.

I hope you are building your own treasure box of God's precious promises. They will keep you from drowning when the storm inevitably comes.

3. *The surety of His provision.*

The apostle Paul understood what it meant to live with a little as well as a lot. In Philippians 4:11 he shared the secret to surviving seasons of leanness. Here's what he said: "I have learned in whatever situation I am to be content."

Paul was in prison when he wrote that verse. It was also in prison that he wrote: "My God will supply every need of yours according to his riches in glory in Christ Jesus" (Philippians 4:19). Paul believed in the surety of God's provision. He didn't look at his present circumstances and doubt God. He didn't spend his time worrying about whether his financial cushion was big enough to weather the future economic crisis. He trusted that God will never leave His children in need.

WHAT WE CONSIDER critical to our comfort can often be a hindrance to full freedom and everlasting joy.

The same God who could provide for Paul on the good days could also provide for him in the prison. And He's the same God who will provide for you in your time of need. He's a God who is sure to provide. That's not to say you shouldn't be wise in your finances and in putting money aside for a rainy day. But it is the understanding that God is bigger than your savings. In days of economic unrest and financial instability, I cannot hear this truth often enough. It gives me comfort deep in my anxious soul.

MEANWHILE, BACK IN THE JUNGLE . . .

Though it felt like forever, the morning sun finally peeked through the window of the hut that I was sleeping in. The morning brought with it news of a river a short walk away. The water was clear and cool. There was an outhouse conveniently stationed by the river. We bathed under the warmth of the morning sun and never had to use the bucket toilet. We'd never been more grateful. We'd never felt more free.

Later that day, after every person in the little village had come through the line for medical treatment, we huddled around a fire and shared the story of Jesus. Tears glistened on hardened faces now gone soft. Hearts broke as freedom claimed new lives for eternity.

We had come to the jungle with light bags and heavy hearts, but we would be leaving with hearts full and our bags long forgotten.

God's ways are not like our ways. He sees with a heavenly perspective. He knows the end from the beginning. What we consider critical to our comfort can often be a hindrance to full freedom and everlasting joy.

One final story to end this chapter.

Elisha was a farmer. He was hard at work when God called him. It was a day like any other, as God's call usually comes. It came unexpectedly and without much fanfare. But when it came, Elisha's response was dramatic.

In 1 Kings 19:21, we're told that "Elisha left him and went back. He took his yoke of oxen and slaughtered them. He burned the plowing equipment to cook the meat and gave it to the people, and they ate. Then he set out to follow Elijah and became his servant" (NIV).

In other words, Elisha drew a line in the sand and jumped—all in. He refused to be held back by his oxen and his home. He refused to ever again be tempted to go back to the safety of home. He put his hand to the plow and would never turn back. No plan B or safety blankets. Elisha burned up his oxen, cooked them, and knew that Kansas was forever in his past.

What about you? Are you still yearning for your Kansas? Are you still dreaming of home? Or have you finally figured it out? Kansas is not the place you left behind. Kansas is wherever God's presence is. No matter where you go, and no matter what you do, God's heart is your home.

Three years ago my husband lost his job in a very sudden and ungodly fashion while working in a Christian environment. The loss of his income was a heavy blow, but knowing the pain was inflicted by a Christian organization was even harder to swallow.

We had to sell our home and downsize. I was humbled and began letting go of material possessions. After a lengthy search for a new home and a very stressful move, my husband had major surgery. Yet God showed me that despite our trials, He remained in control and would provide exactly what we needed when we needed it. I learned to be patient during that time.

When I thought things were getting better, one of my children revealed that she had been going through traumatic emotional and physical challenges. Her revelation shocked and drained me. My relationship with my husband became strained. I felt lonely and hopeless. I questioned my value as a mother, a wife, a friend, and felt I was losing my identity.

Then by God's grace I started developing a clearer understanding, and I realized that God was still with me throughout all of my struggles and darkness. God had surrounded me with His Word and His people. All He asked was for me to be still and know that He is God. Oh, how blessed I am because of my trials—Jesus has saved me and will never let me go.

—SUSA

Chapter Six

THIS ISN'T WHAT I SIGNED UP FOR

Lower your expectations of earth. This is not heaven, so don't expect it to be. —MAX LUCADO

In this chapter, we're going to unfold the last layer that God wants to strip from us as we follow Him.

Have you ever turned the water on and stepped into the shower expecting nice, hot water, only to find it freezing cold? Or have you ever turned the hair dryer on expecting it to run smoothly only to find out that the fuse is burnt out?

It's a terrible feeling. It's the weight of failed expectations. You thought your life would be different by now. You thought you'd be married or already have a couple of kids. Perhaps you thought you'd be in your dream job by now and your life would be well on its way. You thought married life would be different, richer; instead, you spend your days driving little people to many places, still wondering about the meaning of life and frustrated with, well, everyone. Is this the life God intended for you? Is this all there is?

My struggle with failed expectations peaked in the years after God called me to full-time ministry. Those years became the hardest years of my life. I recognized that God had gifted me in teaching. I saw early signs of fruitfulness in ministry as God confirmed His call in my life. The small Sunday school class I led soon grew to a vibrant group of young professional women, hungry for God's Word. I enjoyed putting lessons together, and the students ate up the material. I started writing a weekly newsletter at that time, and saw the Lord use yet another area of giftedness for His glory.

For a short while, I sensed God's blessing and approval like never before, and I loved it. Though I may have been too humble to admit it out loud, like so many other young Christian women gifted in teaching, I thought God was raising up the next Beth Moore. It was only a matter of time before the world noticed me.

I completed my fellowship in pediatric emergency medicine around that time and started looking for a place to work. I had it all figured out. I would stay in the church where God was making it obvious to everyone how gifted I was. I would find a part-time job to support myself and serve God with the rest of my time. Boy—was God lucky to have me.

I expected God to deliver. I expected God to open doors for me. I expected success, greater fruitfulness, and all kinds of blessings to honor the sacrifices I had made for Jesus. Instead, before I knew it, God had transplanted me to Chicago, where the winters are long and the cold is piercing. God had just plopped me in the wilderness familiar to all who have ever heeded His call.

Instead of wide open doors, I got used to the sound of them slamming shut in my face. Soon the initial glow of my "yes" to God's call turned into a senseless repetitive prayer that sounded a little bit like this: "Why me, Lord? Why me?"

While I had expected Him to use me, He was committed to making me usable. While I had expected Him to honor my obedience, He was committed to making me honorable for His sake. While I had expected outward results, God was interested in internal heart change.

Disappointment occurs when our destiny doesn't line up with our dreams. One of the greatest crises in our faith will take place when our hopes seem to fail, our dreams delay, and we think God is unaware of how terribly hurt we feel. If God can do anything, we reason, and doesn't, then He must not really care. And if God can't do anything about our situation, then is He really God at all? As the questions linger, the distance separating us from the Lord widens until we hardly recognize Him anymore.

> **JESUS IS NOT** the means to an end toward our version of the American dream.

It's a dangerous place to be.

God warns us against putting our hope in circumstances and in fairy tale endings here on this earth. Most of us are confused about the gospel. The gospel of Jesus Christ is not that by getting Jesus, all of our problems are going to be fixed and our dreams will come true. Jesus is not the means to an end toward our version of the American dream. No. The gospel of Jesus Christ is that we get Him, and by getting Him we get everything, and with Him in our life we can face any circumstance that comes our way, with joy and confidence and the knowledge that He is enough. It is only as our own human expectations are destroyed and radically transplanted by the truth of Jesus Christ that we will find in Him the answers we are desperately seeking and the joy we long for.

Moses understood it. His dream had been to go to the Promised Land. He never did, but only stared at it from afar. David wanted to build a house for God. He didn't. Job expected God to keep disaster from him. We all know how Job's life played out. Then there's John the Baptist, the greatest man who ever lived by Jesus' claim. He was thrown in prison for speaking truth to Herod. Though he may have wanted to be delivered from prison, John's head was chopped off instead.

Wrong expectations are common, and they are toxic to the life of the Christian. When God calls us to Himself, He commits to removing those wrong expectations and replacing them with what He knows will bring us freedom.

IDENTIFYING WRONG EXPECTATIONS

There are four common expectations that we are tempted to place our hopes in that will fail us every single time. I'm going to use Joseph, the guy with the amazing Technicolor dream coat, to point out these wrong expectations.

Joseph was one of the good guys. He was the son of Rachel, Jacob's true love, arriving after years of barrenness and waiting. One day he had a dream. He dreamed that he would be great and would rule over his brothers. He probably shouldn't have told his brothers that dream. But he didn't want to lie; he really did have that dream.

It didn't help that Joseph's father loved him just a little bit more than he loved the rest of the dozen and had given him that great coat. That Joseph wore it every chance he got didn't help. It was a recipe for disaster.

Joseph had expected to rule over his brothers. They threw him in a pit instead. Joseph thought that God had a plan for him that included greatness. He became a slave in Egypt instead. Life took a devastating turn for this kid from the 'burbs of Canaan. He was about to enter a long and difficult wilderness. The truth is that Joseph handled his time in the ensuing wilderness with far more grace and acceptance than any of us would, but his story brings out four wrong expectations that we tend to place our hopes in:

1. Immediate fulfillment of our dreams.

We all have dreams. We can't help it. It seems inevitable that His call will come with some pretty serious dreams and some pretty high expectations. I mean, He's God. The sky isn't even His limit!

When I sensed God's call to ministry in my life, I assumed that because my dreams were now God-type dreams, they would be fulfilled at a steroid-fast pace. If what I wanted to happen happened, I felt happy with Jesus. If I ran into unexpected delays, I became disenchanted with the Lord. I started questioning God's call. If He'd really called me, wouldn't He prove it by providing more evidence of it in my life? Others were doing great things for God while I sat shackled in my own pit, waiting for God to show up. Pretty soon I went from doubting God's call to doubting God Himself.

I became resentful of God's ways.

I've already told you how God used the waiting period to strip me of my pride and self-righteousness, but God still had to strip me of my expectations and my dreams. His goal wasn't to hurt me but to protect me. Dreams come and go, but God never leaves. Dreams change, but God is constant. Dreams are temporary, but God is eternal. Until I learned to want Him more than I wanted my dreams, I was setting myself up for disappointment.

Delays are not an indication that God has abandoned us. Sometimes delays simply mean that we need to change. I needed to change. My dreams had become my idols, and it was time for that to change.

The world tells you that if you work hard enough and chase your dreams diligently enough, anything can happen. God's way is the opposite. It is only in giving up your dreams to the Giver of dreams that you will find true joy and satisfaction. God's grace is willing to do whatever it takes to show you that a dream—no matter how godly it may be—is just a dream and must be let go.

2. Visible fruit for our obedience.

Joseph was as honest a man as you could find. He was faithful and hardworking. He didn't have a lazy bone in his body. To top that off, he was a looker. The guy had it all. Even more amazingly, he seemed to always do what was right. When his father wanted him to deliver a meal to his brothers, he did it without complaining. In return, he was sold as a slave to a passing caravan. Undaunted by his fate, Joseph remained obedient. He became chief-something under Potiphar. When Potiphar's wife tried to seduce him, Joseph didn't succumb to her wily ways but ran fast. He got thrown in jail for it.

I SPENT TEN years of my life looking for a reward for my obedience to the Lord.

Here was a guy who knew the Lord, kept doing what he

was supposed to, but looked like he was being punished for it. It didn't seem fair.

I spent ten years of my life looking for a reward for my obedience to the Lord. I had made wise choices as a teenager and as a young adult. I hadn't had sex, and I repented of evil thoughts quickly. I read my Bible every day. I committed my life to serving the Lord. I expected God would honor my obedience with results.

The harder I looked, the less I saw and the more I became disappointed in the Lord. If you're looking for visible fruit as a sign of God's favor, stop looking right now! God is far more interested in developing the fruit of the Spirit in us than He is in producing whatever visible fruit we deem a sign of our success.

3. Ease of our journey in response to faith.

Joseph believed that God had a plan and purpose for his life. But instead of a life of ease, Joseph was catapulted into a life of pits and prisons. Instead of a reward for his great faith, God stripped Joseph of every bit of comfort until he was ready to fulfill God's call in his life.

Landing in the pits when you don't expect it can be confusing. I recently emailed a friend in ministry these questions: Is it normal to feel this level of strain and difficulty in the pursuit of Jesus?

If you're looking for comfort as the measure of the rightness of your decisions in life, you're going to miss it every time. If you're looking for ease as your gauge of God's will, stop it. Comfort and ease are a poor measure of success. Christ's way is narrow and His example is in suffering. In

Hebrews 2:10 we're told that "it was fitting for Him, for whom are all things and by whom are all things, in bringing many sons to glory, to make the captain of their salvation perfect through sufferings" (NKJV). Christ exemplified the life of suffering as the best gauge for success.

Holiness is another great measure for direction. Are you growing closer to the Lord through the suffering you're enduring? Are you more obedient to Him today than you were a year ago? Do you long for more of Him in your life?

The greater the strain you feel today the stronger the faith you will have tomorrow. If you're expecting the road to be easy just because you answered God's call to live for Him, think again. God's main purpose for us is holiness and Christlikeness, not ease and comfort.

4. Deliverance after a time of waiting.

The most flabbergasting chapter in the life of Joseph is Genesis 40. Joseph had been in prison for a while. Two new prisoners showed up: a baker and a cupbearer. One night, they each had a dream. They were in luck because Joseph's specialty was dream interpretation. Sure enough, Joseph predicted exactly what would happen. He had asked only one favor in return: Don't forget me when you're out.

It's not hard to see how Joseph's expectations were raised. It's not hard to sense the joy he must have held on to, knowing his deliverance was on the way. Tragically—or so it seemed— the baker was killed, and the cupbearer forgot about Joseph.

Joseph's spirit could have been crushed. His hope for deliverance after a time of waiting evaporated into thin air. Was God real? Was obedience and faithfulness worth it?

God uses the waiting to sanctify us and transform us. We've talked enough about the waiting process by now that you should be nodding your head in agreement. But what most of us need to remember is that God is the One who determines when the waiting will finally end.

I know all about bakers and cupbearers. The moment I run into one of them, my expectations run off with hopes of deliverance. Surely this is from the Lord. Surely the answer is on the way. Placing my expectation in a cupbearer will only lead to disappointment. Only the Lord is worthy of my hope.

> **ARE YOU MORE** obedient to Him today than you were a year ago?

People will always crush our expectations. They can't live up to what we want. To expect that from them is not fair to them. They can never meet our needs. We must stop getting caught in the cycle of looking to them for help in time of need.

GREAT EXPECTATIONS

Two more years passed while Joseph remained in the cold, dank prison cell. But one day, everything changed.

One day, Pharaoh had a dream. No one could interpret the dream. That day, the cupbearer finally remembered Joseph. Of course, this time the timing was perfect. God is always on time. This time, Joseph, the guy with the amazing robe, would finally see his dreams come true. Instead of simply being freed from prison, God had arranged it so that Joseph would become indispensable to Pharaoh. Instead of simply going back to Potiphar's house, Joseph would now save the people of Egypt and of Israel from famine.

The road often gets darker before deliverance comes. But God always delivers His children after a season of waiting and He always does it in His perfect timing. Now that's what I call amazing grace!

So what did we really sign up for?

We've talked about wrong expectations, now it's time to counter that with the kinds of expectations God *does* want us to have.

1. Not my hopes but His presence.

It's a funny thing about God's presence. If you've answered God's call for your life and accepted Him into your heart, His presence is with you and in you forever. Most of the time we don't notice Him, so we forget how near He is.

It happened to two men on the road to Emmaus. In Luke 24:13–27 two men were despondent on their way to Emmaus. They had just seen all of their dreams dashed. The Man they thought would save them had been crucified on a tree. Talk about demolished expectations. Their heads hung low. Their pace was slow.

Suddenly a man came up by them and started talking to them. They didn't recognize him. "We had hoped that he was the one to redeem Israel," they told him (v. 21). We had hoped He'd save us from our mess. We had hoped better days were ahead. "We had hoped" carries a whole lot of disappointment in it.

"O foolish ones, and slow of heart to believe," Jesus answered (v. 25). How dim our vision can be. How small our faith is. Jesus would go on to tell the disciples on the road to

Emmaus all they needed to hear. But more importantly, He stayed near. He remained with them until their eyes were opened and they saw Him for who He really was. He stayed close until they felt His presence nearer than they imagined.

There have been way too many times in my life where I've almost quit. The things I expected God to do after years of waiting and praying looked dismal. I had hoped for results that didn't come. When I looked for others to help me, I came up empty. I finally got to the place where I was ready to see.

Only His presence will bring the healing you need. Run to Him, Christian, and find Him as near as you long for Him to be.

2. Not my dreams but His will.

In Ephesians 2:10 Paul gives God's followers a promise: "For we are his workmanship, created in Christ Jesus for good works, which God prepared beforehand, that we should walk in them."

God has a plan. He has a plan for your life and mine. You may think you know His plan but all too often, you only know what you think you know. The prophet Habakkuk wanted a plan. He dreamed of Israel's salvation. When he didn't see the answer, he questioned God. "O Lord, how long shall I cry for help, and you will not hear?" (Habakkuk 1:2)

Habakkuk thought his dreams were bigger than God's. God's response is humbling. In Habakkuk 1:5 He told his prophet: "Look among the nations, and see; wonder and be astounded. For I am doing a work in your days that you would not believe if told."

God always has a plan. His ways are higher than our ways; His perspective wider than ours. Somehow, by His grace, He allows us to be a part of His plans. The best part of the story is that God graciously gives us His Word to remind us of His plans. We don't have to wonder about it. In Jeremiah 29:11 He tells us: "'I know the plans I have for you,' declares the Lord 'plans for welfare and not for evil, to give you a future and a hope.'"

Our dreams are part of God's will. We didn't create our own dreams. He gave them to us. His promise to us in Jeremiah 1:5 is this: "Before I formed you in the womb I knew you, and before you were born I consecrated you." In Isaiah 46:11 He says: "I have spoken, and I will bring it to pass; I have purposed, and I will do it." And in Psalm 138:8 He promises to perfect that which concerns us.

Our foolishness begins the moment we place our expectations in our dreams instead of resting fully on the Lord and His promises. Have you gotten to the place in your life where you can say what David said in Psalm 62:5–6: "My soul, wait silently for God alone, For my expectation is from Him. He only is my rock and my salvation; He is my defense; I shall not be moved" (NKJV).

In my darkest hours in the years following God's calling me to vocational ministry, I got to the place where all I had to hang on to was God's Word of promise. During those years I found out that when God's Word is all you have, His Word is all you need. His promises are true and everlasting. His Word will never fail you.

Stop trusting your own feelings. Stop looking to your own desires. It's time to rest your hope fully on God's promises.

3. Not my strategies but His ways.

Once in a while I see a patient who comes into the ER with a complaint. I diagnose the problem and send the patient on his way with a plan. A few days later, he comes back to see me—again. We call those guys "bounce backs."

"What's wrong?" I ask.

"Nothing has changed. I'm still sick," comes the frustrated answer.

"Well, were you able to keep the medicine down?" I ask.

"The medicine? I didn't take the medicine."

It's at that point that I feel free to give the guy a lecture. See, you can't dream of getting where you want to go until you decide to give up your own strategies and embrace the ones that work.

As a follower of Jesus Christ, only His strategies will lead you to success. You don't have to work harder, you don't have to wonder why. It's time to let go of your own strategies and rest in His ways.

Godly goals can only be accomplished with godly strategies. Godly strategies encompass His ways, His timing, His fruit, and can only be done by His strength. He determines the right outcome measures for your life. He sets the timing for your waiting.

You can draft all the strategies in the world and expect them to work, but if you're a child of God, only His strategies will yield lasting fruit. Are you fully surrendered to His way in your life? Are you placing all of your expectations in Him?

BE FREE

So how do I make it happen?

We've established that God's plan is to strip us of wrong expectations. We've identified some godly expectations. It's time to summarize four easy steps to live in the freedom of God's will.

1. Stop listening to the lies of the culture.

Lies are so easy to believe. Satan is a liar, and he is determined to discourage Christ's followers. He often uses our culture to shove the lies down our throat: "Dream big, do more, be all you can be, you deserve to succeed." While there may be nothing inherently wrong with some of these claims, they can become tragic when we rest our hopes on them.

When I face big disappointments in my life, it's easy to believe that God doesn't really care about me, or that He can't do anything to change my circumstances. It's easy to believe that God has forgotten about me, or that He loves others more than He loves me. In those moments, I've believed lies about who God is. It's time we reject these lies for good.

WHAT SATAN will use to defeat us, God will use to transform us.

2. Start living by the truth of God's Word.

God's Word is true. His character is true. His plans for us are sure and secure. He keeps every promise He makes, and He never lies. He is a shield for those who take refuge in Him (Proverbs 30:5). His way is perfect. Instead of believing the lies that constantly hammer our heads, we've got to learn to default to God's Word of truth instead.

Rest comes when we embrace the truth that God loves us and is in control of our life and future. The moment we identify the lies we believe, we must quickly replace them with the truth of God's Word.

3. Get over your obsession with dreams.

Maybe your dream is to save the world by the time you turn thirty, or to preach in a church filled to capacity. You want to win the world for Christ. You've got good goals. They're godly goals. Now all you need is Jesus to make them happen.

It's time to get over yourself. I'm not being mean or harsh. I've had to apply this principle in my own life. God has a perfect plan that's personally tailored for your life. It's only as you get over your obsession with your dreams and learn to be obsessed with our Savior that you will find lasting freedom.

4. Surrender to the process.

God's process always includes waiting. His process includes hope in the darkness.

Lamentations 3:31–32 says: "For the Lord will not cast off forever, but, though he cause grief, he will have compassion according to the abundance of his steadfast love." You are not forgotten. Your circumstances will eventually change. Learn all you can from them now, and when it's time, be ready to receive God's goodness.

You don't have to continue in disappointment. God is good and He is in control of every detail you are facing.

Are you still hung up on the fact that you asked God for something once and He didn't give it to you? Are you still having your version of an adult temper tantrum? Perhaps God didn't answer you the way you wanted Him to because He has a better plan for your life. Maybe He knows you better than you know yourself.

What Satan will use to defeat us, God will use to transform us. Joseph understood what I typically forget: What others mean for harm, God will use for our good. Joseph saw God's hand in every difficult detail of his life. When given a chance to vindicate himself and get back at those who had wronged him, here's what Joseph said: "You meant evil against me, but God meant it for good, to bring it about that many people should be kept alive, as they are today" (Genesis 50:20).

Are you wondering when you'll finally see deliverance from your prison cell? It's coming. God is in the process of working all things together for your good and His glory. Until then, stop asking why and start asking *what*. What is God trying to strip from you?

Could it be that you just need to readjust your expectations?

I married my best friend on December 21, 1997. We were so in love and spent many nights talking, laughing, and traveling together. He was a godly man and continued to show increasing spiritual growth in his life. He grew in the knowledge of the Savior and took servant leadership challenges with our church. Our life was perfect.

On our first anniversary weekend we took a trip to the House on the Rock. On our ride home on December 22, 1998, we hit black ice and my life was forever changed. Steven went home to be with his heavenly Father.

Many questions came to my mind in the months that followed the accident. Why did God take my husband home on our anniversary date? Why did God take him home when he was really beginning to grow? Why has this tragedy happened to me?

I still don't know the answer to these questions, but I'm reminded of our human frailty and of God's greatness. Psalm 102:11–12 says this: "My days are like a shadow that declines; and I am withered like grass. But you, O Lord, will endure for ever; and your remembrance unto all generations."

—ANGI

Part Three

MOVING PAST THE PAIN OF BEING STRIPPED

Chapter Seven

DON'T STOP BELIEVING

Faith never knows when it is being led, but it loves and knows the One who is leading. —Oswald Chambers

S o far we've focused on what God wants to remove from our lives in order to make us more usable for His service and in order to draw us closer to Himself. Many of you have felt the pain of being stripped, or you may be feeling it right now. You're going to love the direction we're about to move toward. From this point on I'd like to address how to move past the pain of being stripped.

In other words, it's time for some healing! Sooner or later, no matter how many layers of skin are debrided off a wound, healing will slowly begin and new skin will finally grow back. God's plan is to invariably replace the dead skin with new and healthy layers of faith, grace, prayer, and endurance.

I've been working out with my trainer for over a year now. I show up faithfully once a week for the forty-five-minute session. I bend and I hop. I lunge and I lift. No matter how hard I work at it, when I look down at my abs, they seem to be just as flabby as when I first started.

My faith muscles often feel like my abs. No matter how hard I try to grow them, they remain mushy and weak. When turbulence comes, my faith muscles still get shaky at best.

God doesn't want us to live with wobbly faith. His plan is for us to be confident and secure in Him. Did you know that the word "faith" is mentioned over two hundred times in the New Testament alone? We are saved by faith. We answer God's call by faith. Just about everything we do in the Christian life involves faith. In Hebrews 11:6 we're told that "without faith it is impossible to please him." Yeah, faith is a big deal to God.

Let's go back to Habakkuk. We've mentioned him a few times already. He was a man who looked for answers and learned to wait. In Habakkuk 2:4 he gives us some more insight into the Christian walk. He says: "Behold, his soul is puffed up; it is not upright within him, but the righteous shall live by his faith."

Let me explain a few words before we go on. The word "righteous" simply means those who have embraced Jesus Christ's righteousness as their own by faith. In other words, if you're a born-again, saved follower of Christ, you are righteous.

I also want to define the word "faith." My favorite definition of faith is one my church often uses: "Faith is believing God's Word and acting on it, no matter how I feel, knowing that God promises a good result."

I have observed a pattern in my life that is common to many followers of Jesus Christ. Though I have readily embraced Christ Jesus as my Savior by faith, I find myself stumbling when it comes to faith in my day-to-day life. I know I'm not alone in this struggle.

I'd like to pick on none other than Abraham as a great example of a man who lived by faith most of the time, but blew it in a big way at other times.

ALL THE WAY BACK TO ABRAHAM

You may know Abraham as a giant of the faith, and he certainly was that. But when we first meet him in Genesis 12, Abraham wasn't even called by that same name! He was Abram, a man whose father worshiped idols in the land of Babylon (Joshua 24:2). One day, God called Abram to Himself, and the rest, as they say, is history.

Abraham obeyed God. Hebrews 11:8 tells us his story: "By faith Abraham obeyed when he was called to go out to a place that he was to receive as an inheritance. And he went out, not knowing where he was going."

"Not knowing where he was going." In other words, Abraham started walking with his eyes blindfolded. That's pretty incredible faith. Abraham was so convinced of God's call in his life that he picked up everything he owned and was willing to start a whole new life—by faith, without even knowing where he was going. His example is so inspiring. It's how every follower of Jesus Christ should long to live.

FAITH IS EASY when the waves are still and the sun is shining.

One would think that Abraham would be rewarded with some outward sign of blessing. One would think that life would get easier for Abraham after his willingness to radically obey the Lord. But one would think wrong.

Soon after Abraham moves from Haran toward the Promised Land, with only God's word as his backup, he faces an unexpected famine. Surprisingly, instead of continuing in faith, Abraham's faith muscle wavers. He succumbs to fear.

He moves to Egypt and lies to Pharaoh about his wife, Sarah. Only God's goodness and grace saves Abraham in this moment of fear and weakness. The incident reveals this giant of the faith to be just as prone to fear as you and I often are.

REASONS WE LOSE OUR FAITH

Are you wondering how Abraham could go from faith-filled giant to fearful coward in a matter of a few verses? I'd like us to consider four reasons why most of us tend to lose faith in the Lord:

1. We run into unexpected, difficult circumstances.

It was the famine that changed everything. Life was going smoothly for Abraham until the famine hit. Faith is easy and belief is possible when the waves are still and the sun is shining. We've all been there. Life is good until the storm hits and famine settles. The disciples went into panic mode the minute the storm began, despite having Jesus in the boat with them. And you and I routinely abandon the road of faith at the mere sight of unexpected turbulence and difficult circumstances.

The thing about famine is that it's painful and hopeless and makes people desperately hungry. Most of us can handle a day without eating, but the idea of a famine will send us into a tizzy. We expect circumstances to be somewhat difficult in response to God's call in our lives, but it's the level of difficulty that takes us by surprise.

Famine comes in a variety of shapes and colors. If you're single you could be facing a relationship famine without any hope of deliverance. Your famine could be financial or physical. Regardless of the reasons for your famine, you're tempted to wonder when your next meal is coming.

What do you do when your circumstances become unexpectedly difficult? God's plan for us in times of famine is to turn to Him for our sustenance and food. He uses the famine to teach us dependence on Him. When the Israelites were stuck in the wilderness, God gave them daily manna to fill their hunger. It was their job to gather it daily and be grateful for it instead of complaining about how bland it was.

Is your faith growing in time of famine, or are you turning to your own wisdom for your solutions? Are you gratefully feeding on God's Word, or are you sick of the same old manna? Faith refuses to cave under the weight of unexpected turbulence.

2. We notice seeming contradictions to God's promises.

The most difficult tests of faith I have faced are ones that come at the heels of God's incredible promises. Oswald Chambers had a lot to say about this kind of valley:

> We have all experienced times of exaltation on the mountain, when we have seen things from God's perspective and have wanted to stay there. But God will never allow us to stay there. The true test of our spiritual life is in exhibiting the power to descend from the mountain. If we only have the power to go up, something is wrong. It is a wonderful thing to be on the mountain with God, but a person only gets there so that he may later go down and lift up the demon-possessed people in the valley. We are not made for the mountains, for sunrises, or for the other beautiful

attractions in life—those are simply intended to be moments of inspiration. We are made for the valley and the ordinary things of life, and that is where we have to prove our stamina and strength.[5]

God's voice sounds clear on the mountain. It's easy to hang on to God's Word when the noise of life is dim and the air is clear. It's when we get back down to the valley with its chaos that our ears strain to remember God's call. Yet it is in the valley that our faith is built. It is in the valley that our strength grows.

Let me give you a practical example of this point: I recently pledged to give an amount of money to God. I sensed God's leading and His Word confirmed it. I expected Him to faithfully provide for my big step of faith. At first, it felt great. I was setting myself up to see God work on my behalf. Then I got an unexpected bill. Then another. I wanted to panic. I regretted my decision to give. I wondered if I should stop tithing for a while.

THE SEEMING contradictions to God's promises when we first take a step of faith will soon crumble and fade.

Until, by God's grace, I remembered Abraham. I remembered how the famine hit the moment Abraham took off for the Promised Land. And I decided to wait by faith. I didn't see any big changes at first, except in my heart. I worried less. I felt joy. Soon I got an unexpected gift in the mail. Then another. You see where I'm going with this.

God is always true to His promises. If He says He will provide every need of ours according to His riches, He will (Philippians 4:19). If He promises to multiply our seed for sowing, He will (2 Corinthians 9:10). The seeming contradictions to God's promises when we first take a step of faith will soon crumble and fade, and God's Word will always come to pass.

3. We misunderstand God's silence.

It's easy to go when someone points the way. It's easy to do when someone tells you what to do. It's the silence that throws us for a loop. Why doesn't God speak when we ask Him to? Why does He seem so far up in the sky when we look for Him?

Abraham had no trouble packing his bags and moving when God said go. He even built an altar after seeing God in a dream. It's easy to soar when you have visible evidences of God's presence and hand in your life. Trouble hits when God seems silent.

When famine hit and God didn't magically provide a tray of food, Abraham wondered. When years went by, and Sarah was still barren, God's promise felt like nothing more than a forgotten dream instead of the divine promise Abraham once heard. If only God would just say something.

Do you find your faith wobbling because God is silent? Are you wondering why He just won't speak?

Preachers rightfully tell us that God's silence is sometimes a result of our sin. They point to Isaiah 59:2 and prod us to confess all known sin in order for our sense of intimacy with the Lord to reappear. I've certainly experienced my share of God's silence as a consequence of my sin. If your season of silence is due to sin, get on your knees right now and take care of business with God. But consider that God's silence could also be a sign of His grace. Oswald Chambers is one of my favorite Christian authors. Here's what he says about God's silence:

> Has God trusted you with His silence—a silence that has great meaning? God's silences are actually His answers. God will give you the very blessings you ask if you refuse to go any further without them, but His silence is the sign that He is bringing you into an even more wonderful understanding of Himself. Are you mourning before God because you have not had an audible response? When you cannot hear God, you will find that He has trusted you in the most intimate way possible—with absolute silence, not a silence of despair, but one of pleasure; because He saw that you could withstand an even bigger revelation. If God has given you a silence, then praise Him—He is bringing you into the mainstream of His purposes.[6]

If you're experiencing the grace of God's silence today, be joyful. You may be closer to the Father than you think.

4. We become paralyzed by our self-centered fear.

The story of Abraham is fascinating for a number of reasons. Here was this man who was married to a beautiful but barren woman, Sarah. God called him to Himself and promised him a child. Abraham followed. Yet at the slightest prospect of danger, Abraham was willing to sacrifice said wife for the sake of his own safety.

In other words, Abraham was motivated by fear. Fear takes over when our eyes drift away from the Lord and get fixed on our own circumstances. Fear takes over when we try to fix our problems without the Lord. Fear takes over when we act instead of wait, when we plan instead of pray, and when we move without asking.

Is your life characterized by fear or do you restfully believe God's promises? The answer may have bigger implications than you think.

I've never thought of myself as the fearful type. I live alone and run a busy children's ER. I can handle just about anything. So when it comes to spiritual matters, it's disconcerting how fearful I get.

I'm afraid of what people will say. I'm afraid of looking like an idiot. Why don't I just stick to my day job?

If I got a nickel for every time I threatened to quit the ministry and move to Tahiti, I could have retired by now. Were it not for God's grace and the encouragement of my brothers and sisters in Christ, I'd be paralyzed into inaction by my fears.

Do you resonate with this kind of fear?

How in the world can we consistently live by faith in the face of difficult circumstances, barren deserts and famines, seeming contradictions to God's promises, and crippling self-centered fear? How do we keep from taking matters into our own hands and trying to make something happen when nothing seems to be changing in our life?

HOW TO LIVE BY FAITH

If you're longing to live by faith and move past the pain of being stripped, you better listen carefully to this next section. Everything in the life of the Christian is meant to make us more Christlike and to grow us in unflinching faith in the Father. Here's how to do it.

1. Turn your eyes away from your circumstances.

When I get ready to sew a kid, the first thing their parent will say is this: "Don't look at her, turn your head away." Those parents are smart. They know that watching me stick a needle in the wound is a lot worse than just feeling it.

You may agree with my assessment or not, but the truth is that the first step to living by faith is to intentionally turn your eyes away from your own circumstances.

There's a great biblical illustration of this. It's in 2 Kings 6. Elisha is with his servant, getting ready to take on the king of Syria. How in the world could a prophet ever take on an army and expect to win? The servant rightfully panics. Here's how the story goes:

"When the servant of the man of God rose early in the morning and went out, behold, an army with horses and chariots was all around the city. And the servant said, 'Alas, my master! What shall we do?' He said, 'Do not be afraid, for those who are with us are more than those who are with them.' Then Elisha prayed and said 'O Lord, please open his eyes that he may see.' So the Lord opened the eyes of the young man, and he saw, and behold, the mountain was full of horses and chariots of fire all around Elisha" (2 Kings 6:15–17).

Most of us need new vision. We need to turn our eyes off of our own circumstances and fix them on the Lord. We need to pray the same prayer that Elisha prayed for his servant: Lord, open our eyes that we may see. The old hymn said it like this: "Turn your eyes upon Jesus, Look full in His wonderful face, And the things of earth will grow strangely dim, In the light of His glory and grace."[7]

> **THE FIRST STEP** of living by faith is to intentionally turn your eyes away from your own circumstances.

2. Do the things you know to do.

I grew up listening to the story of the guy who could walk on a tightrope over the Niagara Falls. People flocked to see him do it from all over the world. It's told that the man would ask people before his stunt: Do you believe I can do this? They would unanimously answer yes. Of course the true test of faith would come when the man asked for volunteers to get in a wheelbarrow while he pushed them across.

You can imagine the responses. "Um . . . I think I'll pass." "Um . . . I think I'll just sit this round out." Faith isn't faith until it acts. You can talk about believing God, but unless you do what God says, you're fooling yourself. James says that if you're a hearer of God's Word and not a doer, you are deceiving yourself (James 1:22).

Maybe you're asking yourself: Well, what promises should I obey? The answer is more obvious than you think. Obey everything you know. Do the things you know to do. Don't complicate life. If you're in a season of waiting, stop wasting your days in self-pity and start looking for people to serve. Get involved in your church. Join a Bible study. Hide God's Word in your heart. You get the picture.

3. Stop living by your feelings.

Feelings are horrible leaders. You can't rely on your feelings to help you do the right thing. When I'm in the ER and a nurse tells me that the patient in Room 1 is looking sicker, I don't listen to my feelings. I act. It doesn't matter if I'm tired and hungry and don't feel like getting out of my chair and walking over to the patient's bed to evaluate him. I do it because it's what I know I must do. Then when I get up and realize I've just saved the kid's life, my feelings soar. You see, feelings are horrible leaders but they're great followers.

One of the biggest problems that Christians face is the habit of living by feelings. When you're mad, you argue and yell. When you're frustrated, you complain. When you feel a sexual urge, you do what feels good. When you're hungry, you eat another pint of ice cream. And when you're tired, you quit.

The life of faith is a life of obedience regardless of how you feel. In order to live by faith you've got to yield to God's Spirit and live by the truth of Galatians 5:24: "Those who belong to Christ Jesus have crucified the flesh with its passions and desires."

THE LIFE OF FAITH is a life of obedience regardless of how you feel.

We are no longer victims of our feelings. We are followers of Jesus Christ. We are dead to sin and self. Christ has overcome our flesh. We are free.

146

So the next time you find yourself hungry and long to see immediate results in your life, the temptation you will face is to give in to your feelings and refuse to obey. Don't do it. There's too much at stake.

4. Keep on waiting on God's promises.

I feel like a broken record talking about waiting on God's promises, but it's truly at the heart of Christ's call to His followers. God does promise a good result for those who love Him. He is faithful and good. He is steadfast and long-suffering. His Word always comes to pass. But it will usually involve a season of waiting.

Abraham had to wait over twenty years before God fulfilled His promise and gave him a son, Isaac. Romans 4:18–21 is a magnificent declaration of what happens when we wait on the Lord. It says:

> In hope [Abraham] believed against hope, that he should become the father of many nations, as he had been told, "So shall your offspring be." He did not weaken in faith when he considered his own body, which was as good as dead (since he was about a hundred years old), or when he considered the barrenness of Sarah's womb. No unbelief made him waver concerning the promise of God, but he grew strong in his faith as he gave glory to God, fully convinced that God was able to do what he had promised.

Abraham got it. He was finally able to move past the pain of being stripped and soar to new heights with the Lord.

RESPONDING TO GOD'S CORRECTION

Hebrews 3:12–13 and 19 is a very sobering passage of Scripture. It says "Take care, brothers, lest there be in any of you an evil, unbelieving heart, leading you to fall away from the living God. But exhort one another every day, as long as it is called 'today,' that none of you may be hardened by the deceitfulness of sin. . . . So we see that they were unable to enter [the Promised Land] because of unbelief."

Unbelief is a big deal to God. The Israelites didn't enter the Promised Land, not because of their sexual sin or because they worshiped idols; as bad as those sins had been, what kept them from the Promised Land was their unbelief.

You may be a seasoned Christian with lots of Bible knowledge. You may be able to share the plan of salvation with thousands. But if you're buckling under the weight of God's stripping process, perhaps it's because you've stopped believing Him. Perhaps you've stopped trusting His goodness and love for you in the midst of your present circumstances.

When God finally gave me an unexpected dream job in ministry, I thought things would get better. God hadn't given up on me. He was showing Himself far more gracious to me than I deserved. But things didn't get better right away.

It didn't take long for me to become disillusioned with life in ministry. I felt discouraged and prone to give up. I expected Christians to behave a certain way, but they often let me down. I compared myself to others in ministry, and found myself working harder and seeing fewer results. The times God did bless me with more fruit, I had a hard time seeing it because I was so caught up in my own negativity. I wanted more results and faster growth. I wanted recognition and my own definition of success. I got tired of trying to "prove myself" in ministry.

Because I had a second job as a doctor, I started dreaming about quitting. Pretty soon, I talked about it. A lot. It wasn't fair to the folks I was leading. I was sinning and I couldn't even see it.

I had completely missed the point of what God was doing in my life. His purpose for me had never been to do more for Him or gain more ground for Him. That was His business. God's goal for me had always been simply to follow Jesus. It was to become more Christlike. The first way to do it was to live by faith—no matter what and no matter where.

God continued to faithfully strip me of pride and fear and impatience and sin; His way was purifying me, but rather than turning toward Him in faith, I constantly threatened to run. Ironically, I had nowhere else to go. It was nothing more than an empty threat to try to get God to do what I wanted Him to do for me.

The key to surviving the stripping process and moving past the pain is not to brace yourself with clenched teeth and white knuckles until it's over. It's in submitting to the Lord by faith.

Faith isn't something that happens to you once in your lifetime at salvation. Rather, it's a daily decision to faithfully take God at His Word and trust Him.

> **WE SERVE A GOD** who is utterly and everlastingly committed to us.

I wish I could tell you that Abraham never messed things up again, but the truth is that only a few years later, Abraham would fall into the same trap of fear again. And once again, God tenderly and graciously delivered him. That ought to encourage us. God doesn't expect us to be perfect, but He does want us to grow.

We serve a good God. We serve a loving God. We serve a God who is utterly and everlastingly committed to us. We serve a God of grace. He is a God to be trusted. He is a God to be loved. He is a God to be believed. Will you run into His arms and rest? Will you surrender to His will, no matter how painful it may seem?

I was stripped from everything when I had a miscarriage and my husband of one year divorced me.

I had been involved with him for six years before we got married. I knew it was not a healthy relationship but didn't want to let go because I had hope that one day we would end up married.

During the six-year relationship, I was growing in my walk with the Lord, and in obedience to God's call for me to remain sexually pure, I gave my then-boyfriend an ultimatum: marry me or break up with me. He married me but served me with divorce papers on our first wedding anniversary.

Needless to say, I was devastated, stripped, and completely broken. I felt like I was in shock. I couldn't even show up to court for the divorce proceedings. I didn't have the energy. I couldn't deal with the rejection, shame, and the idea of being alone again. I hit rock bottom. When you get to the bottom, there's nowhere to look but up. When your dreams are shattered and you're facing the broken pieces, you learn to finally sit still.

It was during these moments of stillness that I saw the glory of God. God in His abundant grace never gives up on His children. He saw me sitting alone, torn, stripped, and naked, and He pulled me up. He reached down and healed my heart. Today, I can confidently say that there was a reason for my painful experience. It was through my darkest moments that the Lord showed me that His grace is sufficient, and I am forever grateful.

—MARISO

Chapter Eight

ALL EGGS IN THE BASKET OF PRAYER

Prayer doesn't fit us for the greater work; prayer is the greater work. —OSWALD CHAMBERS

I've made many mistakes in my life, some more serious than others. Like the time I did a rectal exam without wearing gloves. That was bad. I was only a third-year medical student, but I had a hard time getting over that one. Or the time I replied to the Yahoo! email asking me to verify my account information. That was dumb too. But if I had to boil it down to one thing, I'd tell you that the biggest mistake I've ever made in my life has been trying to execute God's strategies in my own strength.

I'm not the first person to make this mistake.

Consider Jacob, the grandson of Abraham. He had already stolen the birthright that belonged to Esau, his older brother. But that wasn't good enough for him. He then faked being Esau to get the blessing from his blind father. How could he do that to his own aging father?

It shouldn't surprise me though, when I consider my own attempts at manipulating and controlling my own life. I set out trying to serve the Lord until my plans get rejected or thwarted, and I lose it. "What's going on, Lord? Why are You picking on me? Did I misunderstand Your call for my life? Have You forgotten all about me?" I spit out the words and tell myself that that conversation with God was a "prayer."

Prayer. It's a problem for most Christians. It's not that we don't believe in it. It just doesn't seem like it ever accomplishes anything. We'd rather just "do something." If you're honest with yourself, if your life depended on your prayer life, you'd be dead. For many Christians, prayer is definitely the weakest link.

Our problem isn't that we don't believe God can do anything we ask Him. We believe He raised Lazarus from the dead. He gave sight to the blind. He made the lame walk. He let Peter walk on water. He stilled the storm with a glance.

He even rose from the dead.

We believe He can do anything, but when it comes to our day-to-day living, if we're honest with ourselves, the question we cannot escape is this: If God can do anything, and we've already asked Him to, why in the world hasn't He done it yet?

PRAYER. It's a problem for most Christians.

We've been talking about the stripping process that life in Christ entails. We're determined to move past the pain of being stripped. In the last chapter, we learned how faith is the first critical step in moving past the pain of being stripped. In this chapter, I'm going to show you how prayer is the next necessary step needed to thrive in pursuit of the Lord Jesus Christ.

I told you about Samuel earlier in this book. I'd like to

tell you more about his mother, Hannah, as an example of a woman who prayed.

DESPERATE ENOUGH TO PRAY

Hannah had a problem. She was barren. It was a huge deal in her day, and it was made even worse by the fact that her husband, who loved her very much, had a second wife who had plenty of kids. And boy did she rub it in. It was like having vinegar poured into Hannah's wounds day after barren day.

The burden got so heavy that Hannah ended up in the only place she had left to go: on her knees in prayer.

When I do finally pray, I find myself much like Hannah. The main reason I pray is not because I like to do it, and it's certainly not because I have nothing better to do with my time. Often the main reason I pray is that I've finally run out of every other option. My back is against the wall; humans have failed me. I have no other place to go.

Prayer has suddenly become my best option.

God uses the spirit of heaviness brought about by the stripping process to lead us to the only place He knows will satisfy us and bring us peace: the place of His presence.

Have you gotten to the place where you're desperate enough to pray? We tend to look at trials as burdens to avoid. We look for the place where we can check our heavy baggage and travel burden free. Will this road ever get easier? We strive and we strain. We fear and we fret. We mope and we manipulate. We do everything but the only thing that will bring us peace.

When we finally give in and pray, we wonder why nothing happens.

Why is prayer so hard for so many Christians?

We have pages of them. The stack becomes thicker and thicker with time until we eventually give up on it completely. The list of unanswered prayers can be the doom of many Christians.

"I used to pray," I hear people say, "until I noticed that God never answers any of my prayer requests." "What's the point?" others say. "If God really cared about my needs, why hasn't He stepped up to the plate?"

While statements like these seem extreme in nature, they threaten to erode the foundation of our faith to the point of near extinction. Even worse, we've convinced ourselves that we're "praying" when all we're doing is mumbling one-word complaints to a God who feels far, far away from us.

WHY DOESN'T GOD
ALWAYS ANSWER OUR PRAYERS?

It's a question worth asking and a question with biblical answers. I'd like to suggest five reasons why God doesn't seem to answer our prayers.

1. Our prayers remain unspoken.

Many of us talk big but don't deliver. We're good at talking about prayer. We're good at complaining when God doesn't answer. We're good at analyzing and theorizing and intellectualizing our faith, but the last thing we actually do is get on our knees and pray. We know we should. We spend enough time thinking about it. But until we actually start to pray, we will not begin to see God at work in our life in a personal way. Oh, I know what you're thinking. Doesn't God hear our unspoken prayers? Sure He does. I believe His Spirit makes intercession for us with groaning too deep for words when we don't know what to say. But in our case, days will drift by without us even thinking about praying. And then we wonder why God hasn't answered us.

2. We pray for the wrong things.

I work in an ER where kids sometimes come in because they need stitches. If I were to listen to most kids, I'd give them the Band-Aid and skip the shots and the stitches. Their wounds would remain largely unhealed and prone to infection.

But I don't give them what they want. I give them what they need. It's the same way with our prayers. We can ask all we want, but we are blessed to have a heavenly Father who only gives us what is best for us. In James 4:3 it says: "You ask and do not receive, because you ask wrongly, to spend it on your passions." Think about the things you're praying for. Could it be that the Lord knows more about your future than you do and is working things out for your good through His refusals and His delays?

3. We pray the wrong way.

Wait . . . there's a wrong way to pray? Am I supposed to stand up? Or kneel down? How about I lie down? Is there a magic word that I should use? Listen, I'm not talking about superficial methods as they pertain to prayer. I'm talking about praying in the way that Jesus taught us. In the Lord's

Prayer, Jesus gave us a model to use in prayer. We're told to pray to our Father, to pray God's will, to pray in Jesus' name, and to pray for His kingdom.

4. We stop praying too soon.

Our biggest problem when it comes to prayer is that we stop too soon. We give up when we don't see the answers. Job spent many chapters "praying" his problems to God. Abraham prayed for decades until his son Isaac was born. Hannah prayed until God heard. The early church prayed until Peter finally crashed their prayer meeting. Paul prayed until he made it to Rome. Even Jesus prayed in the garden until He found rest. Are you on the verge of giving up? Don't! God often uses delays to increase His glory when the answers do eventually come.

5. We pray without faith.

Did you know that believing God is a condition for receiving? Mark 11:24 says: "Therefore I tell you, whatever you ask in prayer, believe that you have received it, and it will be yours." You've probably filed this verse under the "verses that prosperity-gospel preachers use" category.

FAITH LEAVES the problem at the foot of the cross.

I read this recently: "Prayer without faith quickly degenerates into an aimless routine or heartless hypocrisy."[8] I find this to be true in my life. I often say the words but my heart is not in it. I don't even believe that God will do what I'm asking. So why even bother to ask?

How can you tell if you're praying with faith? Philippians 4:7 gives us an answer: "The peace of God, which surpasses all understanding, will guard your hearts and your minds in Christ Jesus." In other words, if after you pray you find that you're still anxious and worried, if you're still plotting and planning, if you're still complaining and pacing, the odds are you haven't prayed in faith. Faith leaves the problems at the foot of the cross, and the result is a peace that passes all understanding.

WHEN GOD DOESN'T ANSWER YOUR PRAYERS

We left Hannah earlier in this chapter still on her knees, desperate for an answer. She had been stripped of her pride and her ability to fix her own problem. She had been stripped of the help of other people and worldly comforts. She had nowhere to go but down, and nowhere to look but up.

When I find myself in the place where God doesn't seem to be answering my prayers, I must ask myself these three questions.

1. Is it the right time?

They say timing is everything. I have a scooter that my nephew, who is eight, longs to ride on his own. I've told him no so many times I can't keep track anymore. I will continue telling my nephew no until he's old enough to be able to safely ride that scooter on his own. It's not that I'm being mean or that I don't like my nephew. On the contrary, I love my nephew very much, which is why I'd like to see him get past his ninth birthday.

I've had the same situations come up with my patients.

As soon as I admit them to the hospital, they want to know when they can go home. *Not yet*, I tell them. They ask so many times that I get pretty burnt out from giving them the same answer over and over again. I'm not picking on my patients nor do I dislike them. I just know what they don't know: leaving the hospital too soon may lead to their death.

It's seems so logical to explain these principles to you using these examples, yet the moment God doesn't do what I want Him to do, I develop a chip on my own shoulder and stop praying.

When God says no, it may just mean not yet. We need to learn to trust His heart and wait on His timing.

2. Why do I want this?

The greatest question to ask when your back is against the wall is not "*What* do I want?" but "*Why* do I want it?" You may be asking for the right things but with the wrong motives.

I've observed that many of my prayers have my own personal comfort as their highest goal. I may want to see my loved ones come to know Jesus Christ, but it's sometimes simply because I long for peace on holidays and family reunions, or because I don't want to worry about them anymore. I may want my blog to grow because I love Jesus, but I also want to prove to others that I'm good enough and reassure myself that my time isn't being wasted. But what if my writing ended up being merely an act of personal worship to the Lord? Wouldn't that be enough for me? Would I still write as an act of worship to Jesus if I never gained another reader?

Every Christian must stop and ask the question: When you pray for God to act on your behalf, is it for His glory or your own? You'll know the answer by how you react when He doesn't answer the way you want Him to.

3. Where do I need to change?

God often withholds or denies answers to our prayers in order to get us to change. Jonah prayed, but his heart was hard and unchanged. God is more interested in our repentance than He is in our comfort. Is there unconfessed sin in your life? Are there sinful habits you need to break? Is the Lord trying to teach you to be more loving, more patient, more grateful for what He has already given you? God may be using His delays to get you to change where you need to!

> **YOU MAY BE** asking for the right things but with the wrong motives.

Life is hard for everyone. The Christian life is particularly narrow. But we've been given an unbeatable weapon for survival. It's high time we use it.

PRAYER: A WEAPON WITH A STEEP LEARNING CURVE

I often feel like a hypocrite when I pray. Because my prayer life is weak and inconsistent, I often feel like I'm using God to get what I want. I end up praying really lame prayers.

I totally understand emergency prayers. I see patients in the ER when they're really, really sick. "Who's your doctor?" I ask.

"We don't have a doctor," they reply.

"Well how did you end up in the ER today?"

"I couldn't breathe anymore, Doctor."

It's a common scenario. People have poor health care in general, but when faced with an emergency, they know exactly where to find the doctor.

The problem with emergency prayer is that it's awkward. It's like showing up to a family reunion and realizing that you haven't kept up with anyone for the last ten years.

You're afraid to ask for anything that's too personal or anything that really matters because you feel like a stranger in the room. So you resort to small talk. How's the weather? How's the garden? God You're great, God You're good, and we thank You for this food.

We treat prayer like a lifeline when it's really more like oxygen. We need it on a regular basis to survive. Some days we need it more than others, but every day we need at least enough. No wonder God told us to pray without ceasing.

Once in a while you catch someone praying, and you think to yourself: "I want to pray like that." I think about it when I read the story of the poor widow who wouldn't stop knocking on the judge's door until she got her answer. I want to pray persistently. I want to pray patiently. I want to pray fervently, like Elijah did for rain.

Habakkuk prayed like that. He knew God. He poured his heart out to Him fervently and passionately. When you really think about it, every person who was greatly used by the Lord learned this kind of face-in-the-ground, tears-rolling-down, white-knuckled, won't-give-up kind of prayer.

There's a steep learning curve to that kind of prayer, and it is only as God strips us of the things we rely on that we finally learn it well.

I would like to give you three characteristics of prayers that God hears.

1. Not a stranger's prayer.

My nephew can call me anytime of the day or night, and he knows it. I remember when he memorized my phone number. He was two. Once in a while my sister advises him not to bother me because I'm at work, and this is how he responds: "I can call her anytime because she loves me and she told me that I could. I know she'll take my call, even while she's at work." He's right. My favorite calls from him are the ones he makes when he doesn't need anything from me. He'll call me just to say hi.

My nephew calls me because he knows I love him. His response to my love is confidence and reciprocated love. And when he does need a favor, it's hard for me to say no. In fact, I'll do anything within my realm of ability to help make his requests happen.

Confidence grows when love is the anchor. Relationships blossom where communication is present. It's not so different with prayer. God loves you. He died for you. He called you to Himself. He's invited you to call Him anytime. Jesus Christ made a sure way for you to the Father. He's promised you access to the Father. He's sitting at God's right hand, making intercession for you. All you have to do is trust His love and take Him up on His offer. The more you call, the better you'll know Him. He's not a stranger to avoid. He's a Father to draw close to. And He's promised never to hang up on you because He loves you. The amount of time you spend praying will surely reflect your trust in Him.

> **WE TREAT PRAYER** like a lifeline when it's really more like oxygen.

God's Word is clear about this. In John 1:12 we're told, "But to all who did receive him, who believed in his name, he gave the right to become children of God." God adopts you into His family the moment you believe on His name. Do you know the name of Jesus? Do you believe in His name? If you do, then why aren't you praying?

2. Not a passing whimsy.

Hannah didn't pray on a whim. Her request wasn't casually thrown like a coin in a fountain. Hannah was so burdened that nothing mattered to her but access to God the Father. She understood what Paul understood in 2 Corinthians 1:8–10: "For we were so utterly burdened beyond our strength that we despaired of life itself. Indeed we felt that we had received the sentence of death. But that was to make us rely not on ourselves but on God who raises the dead."

Have you gotten to the place in your life where you are burdened beyond belief? I was driving home from work recently when the sobs exploded from my chest. The burden on my heart was so great that I couldn't even verbalize my words, but my sobs reflected the pain I was feeling. I pulled over and cried out to God for the nth time about the problem I was facing.

I found the Lord waiting, and I found immediate relief. The answer to my prayer came soon afterward. It is this kind of explosive prayer that unleashes God's heart to act on behalf of His children.

3. Not the fearful whisper of a doubter.

I'm tired of my tongue-tied, weak-lipped, half-hearted prayers whispered in my feeble attempt to move God to act on my behalf. I'm tired of tiptoeing around the edges of heaven's gates, wondering if I've asked too much, dreamed too big, bitten off more than I could chew. I'm tired of trying to figure out the "right" formula, hoping I've included the "right" phrases, while using the "right" strategy to convince the almighty God that what I'm asking for is not just good for me but for Him too.

I want to be bold in faith. I want to be bold in prayer. I want to be bold in drawing near to the throne of grace with confidence. I want to be bold like the woman in Matthew 15 who was willing to eat the crumbs from the table of the King—like a dog would, desperately, willingly, hungrily, humbly.

Boldness is supreme self-confidence, nerve, sometimes even bordering on obnoxious aggressiveness. I know all about obnoxious aggressiveness; but for a change, I want that obnoxious aggressiveness to show up not in my fighting for my rights, but in my begging for God to show up and do His thing in my life.

I want to be bold because Christ said I could be. I want to be bold because Christ made sure I could be. I want to be bold because it pleases the King. Aren't you tired of insecure doubt-filled prayers that hover around the edges of who God is?

THREE PRAYERS HE WILL ALWAYS ANSWER

I hope you're tracking with me thus far. When God strips us and gets us to a place of desperate need and utter dependence on Him, we finally muster enough faith to pray. If you've been in church long enough, you've heard it said that God always answers in one of three ways: yes, no, and maybe. I tend to dislike "no" answers. I don't care much for "not now," either. The closer I walk with the Lord, the more I'm learning prayers that God always says yes to. Here are three prayers I've learned that God will always answer with a "yes."

1. God—save me.

The Bible says in Romans 10:13 that "everyone who calls on the name of the Lord will be saved." Have you done that yet? Have you called on the Lord Jesus Christ to save you? If you're wondering why God hasn't answered many of your prayers lately, maybe you haven't asked Him the most important question of all.

2. Father—help me.

Again and again throughout Scripture we're told that God delivers the needy when they cry out to Him for help. David made it his habit to cry out to God when in need. In Psalm 34:6 David said: "This poor man cried and the Lord heard him and saved him out of all his troubles." Do you need help in your life? Call out to God. He hears you and He will surely help you.

3. Lord—change me.

Romans 12:2 tells us that God's will is for us to be transformed. God's plan for the Christian's life is to change us into Christlikeness. If you're wondering what God is doing in your life, start by asking Him what He's trying to change in you, and then ask Him to go ahead and change you! That's a prayer God will always respond to!

How's your prayer life going? Are you finding intimacy with the Lord through prayer? Are you seeing Him answer the requests of your heart?

ONE MORE THOUGHT ON PRAYER

Over the years I've found myself a hesitant recipient of God's answers. In other words, when God does answer my prayers positively, I let fear keep me from rejoicing.

You pray because you know you should, but never in your life do you really expect God to answer. That God would answer you seems almost too good to be true. You believe in your head that God hears you, but your heart refuses to make the leap of faith, lest you find yourself crushed with disappointment. But when God does shock you by giving you what you think you don't deserve, you're afraid to believe it. You're sure there's a joke somewhere or that someone's going to pull the rug from under you.

So you hang on to doubt instead. You let fear paralyze you into inaction. You refuse to rejoice lest someone find out that you've been given more than you deserve, that you've been dealt a good hand.

But what if you really did believe the truth that God wants to answer your prayers? What if you really did believe the truth that God has given you more than you deserve? What if you allowed joy to get ahold of your heart as you learned to live by faith that God is all He says He is and more?

The irony is that He's already given us more than we will ever deserve through His Son, Jesus Christ. He's already dealt us the best hand possible through salvation.

WHAT IF YOU really did believe the truth that God has given you more than you deserve?

As Hannah poured her heart out to the Lord, the priest came by and thought she was drunk. She wasn't. Hannah was just praying her heart out. The priest, after seeing her desperation, sent her away with a promise: Your answer is coming. We're told in 1 Samuel 1:20 that "in due time Hannah conceived and bore a son."

Eventually, Hannah got her answer. In time, Hannah saw God's goodness. Prayer was the means for Hannah to see God at work transforming her heart, drawing her closer to Him than ever before.

Hannah's response to God's answer was astounding, but it shouldn't come as a shock. Hannah was so overwhelmed with God's kindness and grace that she still turned around and gave Him back the very thing He'd asked for. Remember Samuel, the kid who God called while living in the temple under Eli's tutelage? Yeah, that Samuel. He was the gift that Hannah gave back to God, and boy, did God ever use him.

Are you putting yourself in the place where you can hear God speak? Are you getting used to the position of humility that is able to receive all that God has in store for you? Are you surrounding yourself with people who will help you hear God's voice in your life?

The thing that will really strengthen your intimacy with the Lord is the sense that He hears you when you pray. Nothing will allow you to move past the pain of being stripped like a daily lifestyle of prayer.

Maybe it's been a while since you've prayed. The answers may be closer than you think. The answers may be just a whisper away.

A FINAL ILLUSTRATION

My all-time favorite illustration on prayer is a story of a man named George Mueller. He knew how to pray and his entire life showed it. This story told about Mueller by a steamship captain will clearly demonstrate a God-honoring perspective on prayer:

> The last time I sailed here, which was five weeks ago, something happened that revolutionized my entire Christian life. I had been on the bridge for twenty-four straight hours when George Mueller of Bristol, England, who was a passenger on board, came to me and said, "Captain, I need to tell you that I must be in Quebec on Saturday afternoon." "That is impossible," I replied. "Very well," Mueller responded, "if your ship cannot take me, God will find some other way, for I have never missed an engagement in fifty-seven years. Let's go down to the chartroom to pray."
>
> I looked at this man of God and thought to myself, "What lunatic asylum did he escape from?" I had never encountered someone like this. "Mr. Mueller," I said, "do you realize how dense the fog is?" "No," he replied. "*My eye is not on the dense fog but on the living God, who controls every circumstance of my life.*"
>
> He then knelt down and prayed one of the most simple prayers I've ever heard. When he had finished, I started to pray, but he put his hand on my shoulder and told me *not*

to pray. He said, "First, you do not believe God will answer, and second, I believe He has. Consequently, there is no need whatsoever for you to pray about it."

As I looked at him, he said, "Captain, I have known my Lord for fifty-seven years, and there has never been even a single day that I have failed to get an audience with the King. Get up, Captain, and open the door, and you will see that the fog is gone."

I got up, and indeed the fog was gone. And on Saturday afternoon George Mueller was in Quebec for his meeting.[9]

Now that's the kind of prayer I long for. It's the kind of prayer I desperately need.

It's time we put all our eggs in the basket of prayer. It's every Christian's privilege and your secret to lasting peace.

The year 2012 was a year of challenge and opportunity for me. My word for that year was "humility," and I got ample chances to learn what humility really is. I lost my full-time job in January. My unemployment benefits ran out in June. The car I had borrowed from a friend had to be returned in July. I found myself with no job, no income, no transportation, and no visible means of support.

It was at that point that I realized all I had was God. I was completely and totally out of resources, but I knew that His resources were infinite. Even though I had no idea how I would find a job or pay my bills, I knew that God had a plan.

My job was to wait on the Lord. I understood that God was using each of those difficult circumstances to draw me closer to Him so that I could see Him, up close and personal, at work in my life.

God stripped me of everything the world holds dear: career, income, savings, transportation, home—and then He showed up with the body of Christ and all His glory. He taught me to be humble, to be transparent, to value relationships, to love Him more, to trust Him alone, and to praise Him at all times through all of my circumstances.

He humbled me and then He lifted me up. By God's grace I didn't give up, and I still praise Him for it today.

—CHARLOTTE

Chapter Nine

BREADCRUMBS OF GRACE ALONG THE WAY

Grace is but glory begun, and glory is but grace perfected. —JONATHAN EDWARDS

I've always loved the story of Hansel and Gretel. What's not to love? Gingerbread houses, a boy and a girl who outwit a mean witch and live happily ever after, reunited with their father in the safety of home. But for me, the best part of the story has always been the part where Hansel and Gretel attempt to leave a trail of breadcrumbs to find their way back home.

I grew up riveted with the idea of a trail of breadcrumbs leading me back home. No matter how lost or far from home I was, all I had to do was trace the breadcrumbs back home, one baby step at a time.

If only life were that simple. But perhaps it's not as hard as we make it to be.

We're talking about how to move past the pain of being stripped. We spent a chapter emphasizing the importance of faith in the life of the follower of Jesus Christ. In the last chapter we focused on prayer as oxygen for the life of the believer. In this chapter, we're going to rest on God's grace. Grace is the difference between the Christian that survives the stripping process who, and the one who feels kicked to the curb. Grace is the difference between the joyful Christian and the miserable one.

GRACE CHANGES EVERYTHING

I love grace. I love everything about God's grace. It's probably best to give you a good definition for grace: grace is undeserved favor. Let me explain.

I tend to speed when I drive. Come to think of it, I tend to do everything just a little bit too fast. Unfortunately, when you're driving, it's not that simple. As you might expect, every so often I get to pull over by the side of the road and wait for the police officer to grant me a reprieve.

I usually get it. I'm sure it's my charming personality that does it, or maybe it's my medical scrubs. But regardless of the reason, I rarely get the speeding ticket I deserve.

Now that's what I call mercy. When I don't get the punishment I deserve, I've been granted mercy. Mercy is great. It comes with relief and joy. Think about this: God saves us because of His great mercy. We deserve death and punishment for our sin, but God in His great mercy saves us by sending Jesus to die on the cross in our place.

Mercy is wonderful and amazing and mind-blowing.

But grace . . . well grace is on a different level altogether. Grace is undeserved favor. Grace is actually getting a reward when punishment is deserved. Grace goes a step beyond mercy.

Think of it this way. Two weeks after the merciful police officer lets me drive away ticketless, I open my mailbox and notice a $25 Starbucks gift card waiting for me. Perplexed,

I open the note signed by the same officer that reads: *Enjoy this cup of coffee on me.*

If you're following my story (which is true by the way), then you understand grace. While mercy is amazing, grace is truly awesome. It is undeserved and good and unexpected, and without grace, moving past the stripping process is immensely difficult.

GRACE IS ACTUALLY getting a reward when punishment is deserved.

Grace is the trail of breadcrumbs that God leaves His children to help us make it all the way back home when we feel lost and confused. Some breadcrumbs are bigger than others. Some are more like big, fat dinner rolls. But for the Christian whose eyes are open, it is these breadcrumbs of grace that offer us hope when the pain of being stripped seems too much to bear.

I recall the first time I connected the dots that something crazy called grace was happening in my life. Don't get me wrong, I grew up learning about grace. I understood that Jesus Christ saves people by faith through grace. I knew that grace was something God gives us that we sometimes offer back to Him at meals.

But the kind of grace that has moved me to my knees is the grace that has pulled me from despair and defeat when I deserved to be left in the pit. When everything around me felt like sinking sand, it was God's breadcrumbs of grace that lifted my head and reminded me that God sees me, He knows me, He loves me, and He will do whatever it takes to get me back home.

HOW GOD REVEALS HIS GRACE

One of my all-time favorite verses on grace is in 2 Corinthians 9:8: "And God is able to make all grace abound to you, so that having all sufficiency in all things at all times, you may abound in every good work."

The verse is pretty much all-inclusive. If you're Christ's follower and are wondering whether you're a candidate for grace, the answer is yes. If you're wondering if your situation is open to grace, the answer is yes. If you're wondering whether you can count on God's grace over and over again, the answer is yes, yes, and yes.

When it comes to grace, God always says yes. God offers us breadcrumb after breadcrumb of grace until we are so full we can hardly bear it. Here are six ways God reveals His grace to us:

1. God's grace through the cross.

The cross changes everything. It stands in the face of what is acceptable and normal and polite. That Jesus Christ would willingly put His life on a cross, suffering pain and humiliation because of His great love for us, is incomprehensible. He was perfect. He spent His life healing people and doing good. He should have been honored and worshiped; instead, by the time He walked up the hill with a cross on His back, He was mocked, ridiculed, spit upon, jeered, and beaten. The Bible tells us in Isaiah 53:7 that "he was oppressed, and he was afflicted, yet he opened not his mouth; like a lamb that is led to the slaughter, and like a sheep that before its shearers is silent, so he opened not his mouth."

The cross was horrific and undeserved. But let me remind

you of His words in John 10:17–18: "For this reason the Father loves me, because I lay down my life that I may take it up again. No one takes it from me, but I lay it down of my own accord."

Jesus Christ, the Son of God, came to earth knowing He would die. He came purposefully to pay the price for our sins. He lived perfectly. He was without sin. He alone is able to stand before a holy God on our behalf. But in mercy He forgave us. In love He saved us. And in grace He gave us far more than we will ever deserve.

Yes, the cross changes everything. Peter understood it. In 1 Peter 2:24 he writes: "He himself bore our sins in his body on the tree, that we might die to sin and live to righteousness By his wounds you have been healed."

Paul understood it. In 2 Corinthians 5:21 he wrote: "For our sake he made him to be sin who knew no sin, so that in him we might become the righteousness of God."

And I understood it as a child when I gave my life to Christ. I understand it more and more each day as I see the depth of my own sin and Christ's willingness to save me.

There's something rather obscene about grace. There's a part of our minds that wants to resist it, to try to pay back for the wrong we've done, to argue that if we do not obey fast enough, we may lose it.

> **THE CROSS** changes everything.

To live without the grace of the cross is to refuse all of God's grace. You cannot grab on to the other means of God's grace unless by His grace you accept God's Son—Jesus Christ. He's the watershed point, the difference between doing it on your own or letting Him be in control. With Him is life. Without Him you're condemned. If you've read this far and still haven't received God's grace, this would be a great time to receive Him into your heart. There is no other way to abundant life.

2. God's grace through His Word.

As a follower of Jesus Christ, engraving God's Word on your heart is your greatest weapon against despair. If you tend to think of grace as a New Testament concept, you are mistaken. Throughout God's Word, men and women have drunk from the fountain of God's grace by resting on God's promises and His Word. Trace it all the way back to Abraham who lived in reliance on God's promises; follow it through to Habakkuk, our favorite prophet, and you'll see a man who boldly and pointedly reminded God of His own promise to His people.

God's Word is resplendent with promises of His grace. His Word points us to the grace of His forgiveness, as well as the grace of His steadfast love and patience toward us despite our sin. His Word overflows with His transforming grace in the life of His followers. His Word is abundant with His grace, granting us freedom from our shame, our guilt, our past, and the inevitable mistakes of our future.

As I pursue God's call on my life, the call to write and speak and teach while maintaining my job in the ER, I continue to be stripped of self-reliance. There are days when I feel weaker and more tired than I have ever felt. During those times, it is the grace of God's promises that keeps me going. When driving to yet another ER shift on yet another holiday,

I remember that in my weakness God's grace is sufficient for me. When I lack the time to adequately (and obsessively) prepare for a teaching, I rest in knowing that God's Word has promised never to return void, and that God will put His words in my mouth when I need them. When I'm not sure what God is up to in my life, I rest in the promise that the Lord gave me at sixteen years old, "That he who began a good work in you will bring it to completion at the day of Jesus Christ" (Philippians 1:6). When I fail to regularly respond to others in patience and long-suffering, I lean on the promise that God's grace can use me despite my failures, and I humbly repent.

God's Word is our confidence that He will do what He has promised to do. His Word is like a drink of cold water on a very hot day. It is like a deep cleansing breath at the end of a very long day. It is our hope in the darkness.

Have you experienced the grace of God's Word? Are you resting fully on the hope that only His Word can give? Jeremiah 15:16 says, "Your words were found, and I ate them, and your words became to me a joy and the delight of my heart."

3. God's grace through His presence.

Most of us suffer from spiritual amnesia. We forget that Jesus Christ is living in us. We have been given the grace of God's person through the Spirit of God living in us. He has promised to be with us always, to never leave us nor forsake us. He has promised to be near us. I catch myself looking up in the sky picturing Jesus Christ as Someone way up there, far from me, peeking through the cloud at my life.

God's presence is far more personal in the life of His children. In Colossians 1:27 Paul says it this way: "To them God chose to make known how great among the Gentiles are the riches of the glory of this mystery, which is Christ in you, the hope of glory." That's as close as someone can get to you. Think of the many times you don't deserve His presence in you, yet He promises to abide in you always.

I'm amazed at how often we live our lives oblivious of God's presence. How much joy and peace we forfeit because we forget that He is near. Unfortunately, most of us are rusty when it comes to practicing God's presence. We aren't well-versed in the language of prayer. We miss the very presence of God because we expect some pie-in-the-sky, touchy-feely kind of experience, when His presence is already ours. We must simply claim it by faith.

4. God's grace though His people.

Earlier we learned that when we depend on people instead of turning to the Lord for help, God will sometimes strip them from our lives. In this chapter, I'd like to point you to God's grace given to us through His people.

I've experienced God's grace in my life through His people more often than I can count. I want to tell you about one such incident. I had been in Chicago for five years, having been called to ministry but with no foreseeable way to accomplish it. I felt like I was stuck in a pit, or at the very least, a snowy ditch.

On a whim, I went to our church's Christmas program. I go to a very large church, and I knew only one other person at that church—my sister. It's hard to meet people at big churches, but I hadn't made it easier for others with my no-nonsense, overly confident façade of an attitude. I remember almost leaving the Christmas program because the room was filled beyond its seating capacity, but by God's grace, I stayed.

It was a turning point in my life.

The church had just hired a new women's ministry director. As she got up to give the introduction, God threw me a breadcrumb of grace. *Talk to her,* I sensed God nudge. *Tell her your story.* Now don't you worry. I didn't hear a voice. There was no light in the sky, although she was wearing white and looked like an angel, but I knew without a shadow of a doubt that in order for me to get out of my pit, I needed to connect with other Christians. In that moment, I sensed the Spirit of God prompting me to take a step of faith and meet this new director. I made a plan I knew she wouldn't be able to resist. I'd offer to serve in any area she needed help with. Though I had felt God's call in my life to teach Bible studies, I was at a point where I was willing to clean bathrooms for Jesus if that was the only thing available to do.

The day of our meeting will forever be etched in my memory. We sat on a round table in a sterile-looking classroom on a random Tuesday morning while I poured my heart out to her. I told her way more of my story than I intended to. I described in agonizing detail how God had been stripping me thus far. I felt naked and exposed but was offered grace to go on. So I did.

That day, a lifelong friendship was born. God had offered me the grace through another one of His daughters. That women's ministry director became instrumental in the next phase of my life in ministry and is one of my best friends today.

Lynne and I still laugh at the strangeness of our friend-ship and how it began. We have very little in common yet everything in common. She likes ruffles and cursive, while I love bold and clean. She hates coffee and I hate Pepsi prod-ucts. But when you look past the surface differences, what Lynne and I have in common is a deep, deep love for our Savior and a hunger to know Him more.

I could tell you story after story of how God has shown me His grace through His people. I'm sure you can do the same. If you can't, start looking for these breadcrumbs. They're all over the place, but I'd recommend starting at your local church. It ought to be a place of grace.

5. God's grace through your circumstances.

We don't typically see "it" when we're in "it." I'm talking about the grace of our circumstances. The circumstances we complain about today will make a whole lot more sense to-morrow. God, on the other hand, sees the end from the be-ginning. He's the Alpha and the Omega, and He knows that the circumstances you are in today are a gift of His grace.

After three years of blogging daily, I was asked to blog for a big national Christian women's group. Trust me, this was already a breadcrumb of grace in its own right. I was pretty excited about it.

But instead of simply being thankful for this great new opportunity, I became frustrated because I assumed that God was about to allow a major breakthrough in ministry for me. I was wrong. Nothing happened except that I had more writing deadlines to keep up with. After a while, I even resented wasting more of my precious time writing for yet another blog.

I almost turned in the towel and quit blogging for them. I wasn't getting much out of the deal. I cringe at how ungrateful I sound, but I'm trying to be as honest as possible.

Why wasn't God doing more godlike things in my life?

I didn't realize that God had a breadcrumb of grace waiting for me around the bend. One day, several months into my blogging for this group, I checked my email and saw a message from a stranger. I almost deleted the message. I'm glad I didn't.

The email was from a woman who is now my publisher. She had been following my blog and wanted to know if I was interested in writing a trade book on singleness. Trust me when I tell you that a person who blogs daily for three years is most definitely interested in writing trade books. By God's grace, a new relationship was born, and Holly is the reason you're reading this book right now.

What I'm trying to tell you is that God's ways may be hard to understand at first. We wrongly interpret our circumstance, and accuse God of not acting on our behalf, when in due time we are able to see the big picture and understand that He's been working for our good all along.

6. God's grace through supernatural means

God reveals His grace through supernatural means. Frankly, everything about God is supernatural. That He loves us and that He died for us is supernatural. That He continues to work in us is supernatural. But there are moments when God chooses the miraculous to show His grace in our lives.

Let me remind you that I'm an average Jane, with an

average prayer life, and a relatively weak faith muscle, but I do believe this: God can do anything, and sometimes He does things that are simply not explainable in human ways.

On rare occasions in my life, He's done that for me. A few months ago I was determined to discontinue my blog. I wasn't joking this time, I was for real. I was frustrated. My life wasn't turning out like I thought it would. I felt like I was wasting my time. I was tired. If God wasn't going to "do" something in my ministry life, I figured I might as well learn how to worship Him on a peaceful beach somewhere.

I prayed about it for a few days and discussed it with my mother. No mother likes to see her daughter struggle, so she agreed that I should quit it. My other close friends agreed too. "You work too hard," they said. "Just relax and enjoy your life." So I sat on my patio with the weight of the world on my shoulders, and I prayed. "Lord, I'm going to stop the blog. Are you okay with that?" It was a simple but faith-filled prayer. Then I waited.

The phone rang. I don't know anyone in South Dakota, but by habit I picked up.

> **SOMETIMES GOD** does things that are simply not explainable in human ways.

"Hi, this is Lina," I said.

"Lina? Oh, I didn't expect you to actually answer. Well, listen, this may not make sense to you at all, but I just called to tell you this: Don't ever stop your blog."

Huh?

I was miffed. I asked for some context. The caller simply told me that he had randomly found my blog while looking for a sermon illustration, had spent an hour or so reading my archives, and felt compelled by God to call me and tell me not to stop my blog. Ironically, he used the business number on my website that no one had ever used to call me before and no one has used since then.

Now that's what I call supernatural grace.

It's the kind of grace that no one can explain. It's the kind of grace that God does because He is God. It's the kind of grace that gives us hope. It doesn't replace God's Word or His presence, but once in a while, God just likes to show off. I'm so glad He does.

Christ reveals Himself to us in many ways. He does it first at the cross. Then He does it through His Word and the certainty of His presence. He does it through His people and the circumstances of our lives. And once in a while when we desperately need it, He throws us a breadcrumb of grace to let us know who's in charge. He's a God of all grace.

SO WHAT KEEPS US FROM ACCEPTING GOD'S GRACE?

I believe there are five main problems that keep us from living in the freedom of God's grace.

1. We are too proud to accept it.

There is a little nugget of a verse in James that says this: "God opposes the proud but gives grace to the humble" (4:6). Pride is a major obstacle to seeing God's grace in your life. You may think you don't need His grace. Or you may think grace is for the weak people who need it more than you do.

Do you think the apostle Paul was weak? Yet he tells of his experience with grace in 2 Corinthians 12:9: "But he said to me, 'My grace is sufficient for you, for my power is made perfect in weakness.' Therefore I will boast all the more gladly of my weaknesses so that the power of Christ may rest upon me."

God allows us to be weak and needy in order to reveal His grace to us. Paul was suffering a thorn in his flesh when he wrote these words about grace. He prayed persistently for freedom from it, but God's solution for Paul was not relief from the thorn, but grace for the road.

If God is humbling you right now, rejoice. A breadcrumb of His grace may be headed your way! God longs to be gracious to us. It's His nature to give grace. As we remain in the place of humility God will see us through to a place of grace.

2. We are too strong to need it.

We just finished talking about Paul and his sense of weakness, but most of us would agree that Paul was one of the strongest people in the New Testament. He endured far more suffering and difficulties than you or I ever will.

If Paul's example wasn't enough to impress you, read this verse in 2 Corinthians 13:4: "For he was crucified in weakness, but lives by the power of God. For we also are weak in him, but in dealing with you we will live with him by the power of God."

In case you missed it, this verse is talking about Jesus. Do you think you're too strong to receive grace? Christ Himself was crucified in weakness. When you feel helpless and alone, God's grace will soothe your weary soul. God longs for men and women who are weak enough to lean on Him. He does

His best work in those who are void of their own strength and will fully rely on His strength.

3. We are too bitter to receive it.

Bitterness is a bigger deal than we give it credit for. Hebrews 12:15 says: "See to it that no one fails to obtain the grace of God; that no 'root of bitterness' springs up and causes trouble, and by it many become defiled."

Bitterness must be rooted out or else it will take over the soil of your heart. You must confess it and repent of it. Do you have bitterness in your heart toward others who have hurt you? Are you bitter toward God because He hasn't done what you wanted Him to? You won't experience God's grace until you let go of that bitterness. The first thing you need to do is to get on your knees and confess it to God. Next, given the situation, chances are you need to make some phone calls and settle some accounts. It's humbling. It's hard. You may feel broken at first. But brokenness is the soil that allows you to receive God's restoring grace.

4. We are too impatient to wait for it.

Sometimes we just give up too soon. We simply don't wait long enough for God to reveal His grace to us. In 1 Peter 5:10 it says: "And after you have suffered a little while, the God of all grace, who has called you to his eternal glory in Christ, will himself restore, confirm, strengthen, and establish you."

GOD'S GRACE will soothe your weary soul.

I often wonder what would have happened had I not

picked up the phone call from South Dakota? Or what if I had skipped the Christmas event at church that year, choosing instead to wallow in self-pity? God's grace helps us remain when we want to escape. His grace strengthens us when we are weak. His grace sustains us when we feel like we are desperately sinking.

"Wait on the Lord; Be of good courage, And he shall strengthen your heart" (Psalm 27:14 NKJV). I know what you're thinking: here she goes again with the waiting. I'm glad you're picking up on the theme. God's grace is revealed to His children in the waiting. Don't be too impatient to receive it.

5. We are too rushed to see it.

We live in a hurry. From the moment we open our eyes until our heads hit the pillow, we are rushed, rushed, rushed. We eat quickly, we spend in a flash, we drive too fast, and we fly by, too harried to appreciate God's wonder of grace. Sound familiar? Martha suffered the same symptoms in Luke 10:38–42.

I've gotten in the habit of blaming the culture I live in for how rushed I am. I've even blamed the city I live in for my hectic speed. It's time we stop blaming our kids and our jobs and our churches for our haste.

God's plan for us includes rest. When Martha asked Jesus to make Mary help her finish the work, she would learn a lesson many of us still need to learn. Jesus' response to Martha was this: "Martha, Martha, you are anxious and troubled about many things, but one thing is necessary. Mary has chosen the good portion, which will not be taken away from her" (Luke 10:41–42). Often the only way to see God's grace is to stop long enough to look for it. Are you creating in your life new opportunities to see God's grace?

I recently started going on a prayer walk. I'm a runner by nature but found that forcing myself to walk slows me down enough to see things more clearly. It gives me a chance to listen. It allows me to process my life and to pick up God's breadcrumbs of grace along the way home.

In the story of Hansel and Gretel, the birds ate the breadcrumbs on their way to the woods. Life has a way of stealing our breadcrumbs of grace if we let it. Satan has a way of stealing our joy. Don't miss the breadcrumbs of grace that God is graciously pouring upon you.

In Psalm 81:10 God gives us this promise: "I am the Lord your God, who brought you up out of the land of Egypt. Open your mouth wide, and I will fill it."

Three years ago I was reading a book by Francis Chan with a small group of women at my church. The book had taken me to a place where I "thought" nothing else mattered but God. I longed to be used by God in a great way. It turns out; I was nowhere ready to be used by God yet. I still needed to be stripped.

A few months after that day, our home burned down. My insurance company accused me of setting the fire. I spent three days in jail and have spent the last three years fighting the court system. God had stripped me of all my comforts, my reputation, and all that I had placed my security in.

I went from having no faith to living on nothing but faith. I went from anger to gratitude. I went from fear to contentment. I can easily look back and see God's hand in every detail of my trials. I'll admit that some days are hard. I don't want to praise God. But other days, I want to stand on the rooftop and shout at the top of my lungs, "God is more than enough!"

—JULI

Chapter Ten

HOLD ON TO YOUR HORSES

Of one thing I am perfectly sure: God's story never ends with ashes. —ELISABETH ELLIOT

Some things in life don't require endurance—like eating ice cream and roller coaster rides. They offer immediate gratification and have very little impact on others. They may be fun but they leave you, for the most part, unchanged. There are other things in life that demand endurance—like running a marathon and making it through medical school. The cost is high but so is the reward.

Endurance is the ability to last in the face of fatigue, stress, and adverse conditions. Endurance is about overcoming mountains and fighting dragons along the way and still coming out alive.

Pursuing God's call in your life demands endurance. Endurance is more than just patience. Endurance takes it a step further. Endurance keeps you going when the going gets tough. Answering the call of Jesus requires both patience and endurance to make it past the stripping process.

I was idealistic in my youth. I thought that endurance was no big deal. If I waited long enough and hoped hard enough, things would work out for me. The older I get, the less endurance I seem to possess. Years and years of patiently waiting have paralyzed my desire to endure and slowed my ability to last. Words like "quitting," "I'm done," and "I'm too tired," have become all too common in my vocabulary. Instead of hoping for more faithfulness, I hope for a permanent vacation in a sunny location. What seemed to be worth the fight in my twenties has become harder to pursue in my forties.

That seems counterintuitive, but God isn't as surprised by my perspective as you'd think. I know because His Word is full of admonition for us to endure. In this chapter, we're going to get a biblical perspective on endurance. If you're like me, often on the verge of bailing, this chapter is going to be good for you.

WHAT STANDS IN THE WAY
OF THE CHRISTIAN'S ENDURANCE?

Sometimes I just need a pep talk—someone to come alongside me, put their arm around me, and tell me to keep on going, that it's going to be all right. When I get in that place and don't see anyone around me to encourage me, I get frustrated with God. Why doesn't God send someone to help me? Why doesn't He make the way easier?

INSTEAD OF HOPING for more faithfulness, I hope for a permanent vacation in a sunny location.

I'm perplexed by how quickly I lose courage and want to throw in the towel. I'm puzzled by how fickle I am after all that God has done for me. How easily I forget Christ's call in my life. He didn't make me any false promises. I knew the road would be hard. He didn't oversell His offer. Tribulation, persecution, suffering . . . I knew what was coming, but I still feel blindsided by the difficulty of the journey. I catch myself dreaming of an easier life. I look for exit ramps leading to quiet streams and lush valleys. Over the years, I've noticed wrong patterns of thinking that have kept me from enduring well.

1. I want what I want, and I want it now.

There's so much pride in this kind of thinking. It's hard to endure when you can't get over your own sense of personal rights.

Remember Samson? He felt entitled to get the wife of his choosing. We've already seen how that worked out for him. King Saul, the first king of Israel, wanted what he wanted the moment he wanted it. Instead of waiting for Samuel the high priest to offer a God-honoring sacrifice, he took matters in his own hands and lost the kingdom because of it. David wanted Bathsheba in a moment of kingly entitlement and destroyed his whole family in the process.

Taking matters into your own hands instead of patiently waiting for God to unveil His will in your life is going to get you in trouble every single time. Trying to accomplish your plans in your own way instead of waiting for God's timing is a sure way to lose your peace and security.

There are no shortcuts to God's will. If you long to move past the stripping process, get used to enduring as long as it takes for God's will to unfold in your life.

2. I'm fallen and I can't get up.

Sometimes sin stands in the way of our endurance. Sin can be besetting. It crouches at the doors of our lives, seeking to disrupt our walk of faith. Avoid it and you will be better set to run with endurance. But allow yourself to be weighed down by sin and the road to heaven will be long and tedious for you.

There was a time in my life when I was easily bogged down by sin. It made me feel hopeless. If I couldn't overcome the sin in my life, how could I ever live out God's call in my life? I felt like a hypocrite and a fraud. My prayers felt weak and God seemed far off. It seemed easier to quit than to live without sin.

I was living without grace. I was trying to earn favor with God through a perfect life. Though I had agreed with the Lord that I needed Him for salvation, I was trying to impress Him with my perfect little Christian life.

I had to repent. I had to agree with God about my sin. Up to that point, deep down in my heart I didn't even feel bad about my sin. I felt justified in it. I felt as if God was partially to blame because He hadn't provided for me in ways that would keep me from sinning. But because I wanted God's favor, I would go through the motion of saying I'm sorry but never really believed that I was wrong. Have you ever done that?

The more God stripped me, the more I was finally able to see the depth of my sin. I started asking the Lord for true repentance. He gave it to me. Instead of feeling hopeless about the future, I started to understand that that very sin in my life was God's grace leading me to greater dependence on Him for my holiness.

Proverbs 24:16 is a verse that has always blessed me: "For the righteous falls seven times and rises again, but the wicked stumble in times of calamity."

If you've fallen into sin—again—and feel like you can't

get up, take heart. God's goodness will surely lead you to repentance. Just ask Him for it.

3. I don't understand why.

Do you ever feel like you'd be able to go on if only you understood why? You don't need to know all the details, but it would help to know why. Why must the road be so hard? Why isn't anything happening yet? Why won't this trial ever end? We waste a lot of energy in the Christian life by asking the wrong question.

Instead of asking why, we've got to start asking *what*.

ARE YOU becoming more like Him?

What is God trying to do in my life through this difficult circumstance? What does God want to change in me through this season of my life?

We get so focused on the tasks in our lives that we miss the heart of God. God cares more about our relationship with Him than how much we're doing for Him. When you consider your life right now, are you closer to the Lord today than you were last year? Do you long for more of Him? Are you sinning less? Are you striving for more holiness? Are you growing in your faith? Are you becoming more like Him?

Romans 5:3 says it like this: "Not only that, but we rejoice in our sufferings, knowing that suffering produces endurance, and endurance produces character, and character produces hope, and hope does not put us to shame, because God's love has been poured out into our hearts through the Holy Spirit who has been given to us."

The greater the strain you feel today, the stronger your

faith will be tomorrow. It's time you stop asking the wrong questions and start answering the right ones.

4. I can't see the light at the end of the tunnel.

What greatly hinders us in our Christian life is the fact that we cannot see the light at the end of the tunnel. We don't see the end of the trial. We don't see what's coming. We say we have faith, but our hearts crave answers today. We say we believe in heaven, but the reality of heaven is nothing more than an esoteric and futuristic concept. The book of Revelation feels too "sci-fi" for our present-day problems.

Is it any wonder that Hebrews 10:36 says "you have need of endurance"?

We need endurance. Paul endured and was able to sing at midnight in the middle of his prison cell. It didn't matter what location he was in, his heart was steadfast in the Lord. Peter endured by falling sound asleep in prison the night Herod had planned to kill him. The angel had to jolt him to wake him and it took him a few more minutes to rub the sleep out of his eyes before he was able to move it. That's how peaceful he was in prison!

These were men who weren't so worried about the light at the end of their earthly tunnels, because their vision had been set aflame with the burning light of God's presence.

Won't you stop looking at deliverance from your trials as the gauge for God's faithfulness to you and see in the midst of your suffering a God who is faithful and true?

He will not rest until He has accomplished His purposes for your life.

HOW CAN I GO ON IN ENDURANCE?

That's a great question. I'm glad you asked it. Let me give you four practical steps to help you go on in endurance.

1. Stop enduring for the wrong things.

I've already expressed my problem of always wanting affirmation. I'm obsessed with analytics and numbers. I suppose most people who have a blog struggle with this at least a little. The problem is that in a performance-based, task-oriented, success-driven culture, it's easy to get carried away with numbers and make them the basis of our success and the reason for our endurance.

I've noticed that when my blog subscribers go up, I conclude that God is blessing me and showing me that I should go on in ministry. If my Twitter followers increase, then I must be on the right path. I measure numbers and book sales and comments and feedback and Facebook likes, never once stopping long enough to ask what it is that actually pleases the Lord. What is God's measure of faithfulness and success? What kind of fruit should we be seeking as a sign of His pleasure?

Human success measures are not God's standard for success. Consider Jeremiah, who spent his life in prison and never saw anyone respond to his lifelong message of salvation. The Lord Jesus Christ Himself looked the opposite of success, humanly speaking, when He hung alone on a cross.

We must learn to endure for godly standards of success or we will remain defeated and depressed. Are you growing in the fruit of the Spirit? Is your life reflecting more love toward those in your life who may not deserve it? Are you noticing more peace in the chaos of your life? Are you growing in self-control, kindness, and long-suffering?

2. Study the Scriptural examples of endurance.

One of the greatest blessings of God's Word is its plethora of people who lived lives of steadfast endurance. This is not accidental. God intended to give us these stories to spur us on to endurance. Listen to these verses:

Romans 4:23–24 talks about Abraham's example of enduring: "But the words 'it was counted to him' were not written for his sake alone, but for ours also. It will be counted to us who believe in him who raised from the dead Jesus our Lord."

In Romans 15:4 we're told: "Whatever was written in former days was written for our instruction, that through endurance and through the encouragement of the Scriptures we might have hope."

In Hebrews 12:1, following the great chapter of the faith, it says, "Therefore, since we are surrounded by so great a cloud of witnesses, let us also lay aside every weight and sin which clings so closely, and let us run with endurance the race that is set before us."

What a blessing to know that God's Word isn't written haphazardly for our occasional perusal. God's Word is a gift, given to us by the Holy Spirit to inspire us to go on, to spur us on toward greater endurance, and to give us hope in our journey home.

3. See in suffering the opportunity to grow.

We whimper at the slightest trial. "Where is God?" we want to know. "Why is this happening to me?" we cry. Do you think you know something about trials and suffering? Consider the New Testament believers. They knew all about trials. They were thrown in prison. They were beaten, spit at, mocked, crucified, killed.

Do you want to know their response to trials? They didn't say "why me?" They didn't doubt God and sink in self-pity. They didn't contemplate quitting. Listen to the words of James, the brother of Jesus, in James 1:2–3: "Count it all joy, my brothers, when you meet trials of various kinds, for you know that the testing of your faith produces steadfastness."

The early Christians understood what you and I are still learning. Suffering leads to growth. Suffering is an opportunity to rejoice. It is the stripping process that makes the man or woman for God. It is His loving hand gently shaping us through painful circumstances that transforms us into the kind of followers He longs for.

Like a piece of metal on an anvil, God's grace shapes us and molds us. Like a piece of clay in the hands of a potter, God's love transforms us. Like silver refined in a furnace, suffering makes us the kind of followers God knows we can be.

4. Surround yourself with balcony people.

The Christian life is all about community. I suppose that makes sense when you consider that God is a Trinity made up of God the Father, God the Son, and God the Holy Spirit. It also makes sense that Christ compares His bride, the church, to a body with many members. We as Christ's followers are members of a family. God didn't save us to live alone. God's plan is for us to grow with one another and to spur one another on to love and good works.

Apart from God's grace, one of the main reasons I am still following Jesus today is that my life is surrounded with balcony people. Balcony people are people who cheer me on when I'm down—and believe me, those days are many. Balcony people are people who help me remember the big picture in life. They're sitting on the balcony, after all, and have a much better view of my life than I do. Balcony people are those who care more about God's will in my life than my own personal comfort. They are people who are more interested in telling me the truth than in agreeing with me.

It's easier to endure when you have balcony people cheering you on. Balcony people don't just show up in your life. You've got to cultivate them over time. You've got to be intentional in finding them. You've got to pray for them. And once in a while, you've got to be a balcony person for them too!

If you're looking for balcony people, the best place to start is your local church.

THE HIDDEN FRUIT OF ENDURANCE

John Egglen had never preached once in his life. Then one day on a Sunday morning in January of 1850, he did. John woke up that morning to a town buried in snow. Surely no one would go to church in that weather. It would have been easy to skip. It would have been easy to stay in the comfort of home. But because he was a deacon, he figured he should go, so he strapped on his boots and walked the six miles to the Methodist church.

Only thirteen people showed up: twelve regular members and a visitor—a thirteen-year-old boy. Even the minister was snowed in. Some suggested they cancel. John almost did.

But because a visitor had showed up, he figured they should stay.

Who would preach? Since Egglen was the only deacon present, the task fell to him. He'd never preached before. He could have said no. But on that snowy morning, he preached. It was obvious he'd never preached before. He drifted and wandered and lasted all of ten minutes. Toward the end of his "message," he surprised even himself with some courage. He looked up, straight into the eyes of the young visitor and challenged him: "Young man, look to Jesus. Look! Look! Look!"

The young man did look and was saved. Years later the boy, now as a man, said, "I did look, and then and there the cloud on my heart lifted, the darkness rolled away, and at that moment I saw the sun."[10]

That young man who was saved was none other than Charles Haddon Spurgeon, who would become one of the greatest preachers of all times.

Little did Egglen know on that morning that his endurance would lead to the salvation of a man who would end up preaching to over 10 million people. Little did Egglen know that his obedience would lead to life for so many.

SOMEDAY, YOU'LL be able to clearly see the fruit of your faithfulness.

You may feel like your efforts are useless and the road unnecessarily difficult. It may be easier for you to give up. But hang on to your horses because someday, maybe soon and maybe not until eternity, you'll be able to see clearly the fruit of your faithfulness.

During my sophomore year in high school, my mother, who was also my best friend, was diagnosed with breast cancer. She was in a growing relationship with the Lord and serving Him faithfully. I thought this "trial" would bring my father to salvation.

After two and half years of battling with cancer, the Lord took my mom home. I couldn't understand "why." Then in the stillness of my soul, the Lord gave me a thought that helped me let go: He is all that I have, and He is all that I ever will need.

—ELIZABETH

Part Four

THE SECRET TO JOY
WHEN YOU'RE STRIPPED

Chapter Eleven

MORE THAN ENOUGH

*God is most glorified in us when we are most
satisfied in him.* —JOHN PIPER

This is probably my favorite part in the whole book. As I
write this chapter, I find myself at a crossroads. I'm forced
to apply in my own life those very things that I'm writing for
you.

There are many things that remain uncertain in my life.
The only thing I know for sure is that one day, many years
ago, God called me to Himself, and my life has not been the
same since. I have good days and I have bad days. I've faced
easy circumstances and difficult ones. I've made friends and
lost others. I've felt the weight of disappointment. But I'm
still breathing.

With each passing day, I find that my idea of God's call
in my life gets vaguer and vaguer, but His face gets clearer
and clearer.

In many ways, we're a lot like Habakkuk. He was living in
a desperate time of great trial and difficulty. His culture was a
mess. His nation was falling apart. The enemy seemed to be
winning. The future looked grim.

So Habakkuk did what every Christian should do. He
looked to God and prayed. He asked the Lord for answers.
In response God gave Habakkuk a vision, or a calling. But

God also warned Habakkuk that the vision wouldn't happen quickly. Habakkuk would have to wait while the vision delayed. Great faith would be needed in the waiting.

Habakkuk kept on praying and waiting. His perspective soon changed. His faith grew stronger.

By the time we get to Habakkuk 3:17–19, his circumstances haven't changed yet, but everything else has changed for him. His mind has changed. His heart has changed. His vision is refreshed. What had begun as a lament over the trials and difficulties Habakkuk was facing finally turned into a song of rejoicing. Read Habakkuk 3:17–19:

> Though the fig tree should not blossom, nor fruit be on the vines, the produce of the olive fail and the fields yield no food, the flock be cut off from the fold and there be no herd in the stalls, yet I will rejoice in the Lord; I will take joy in the God of my salvation. God, the Lord, is my strength; he makes my feet like the deer's; he makes me tread on my high places.

Now do me a favor. Go back and read those verses again. Do it a few times. Immerse yourself in this passage. Soak in it. Understand it. Love it. Know it. Memorize it. Remember it. And allow me to share a few thoughts about this passage as we come to the end of our road together.

I can summarize this passage of Scripture in five words: *God is more than enough.*

He is more than enough. He is more than amazing. He is more than magnificent. He is more than you'll ever imagine or think Him to be. He is simply more than enough.

The word *enough* is a good word. Here's how it's defined in the dictionary: "adequate for the want or need; sufficient for the purpose or to satisfy desire."[11]

We spend our life wanting enough: enough money, enough relationships, enough success, enough impact, enough fun, enough joy. Once in a while, we get enough of what we want, but more often than not we live right beneath the surface of enough—always striving but never quite admitting that enough is, well, enough.

When it comes to the Lord, enough is never enough. That's because He is more than enough. He is more than adequate to meet your wants and your needs. He is more than sufficient to satisfy your desire.

He is more than enough, no matter what you're going through today.

You may be at a crossroads right now. You don't see any visible evidence that God's promises for you are going to come to pass. Or perhaps you've got an important decision to make. Your whole life depends on it. Will you believe that God is more than enough, or will you turn to your own desires and wisdom for comfort? Will you choose His joy, or will you linger in despair and disbelief?

Will you see in Christ the goal of the Christian life, or will you remain entrenched in the futility of what you think will bring you joy? Everything in the life of the Christian flows out of an unhindered and unobstructed relationship with the Lord. Until you learn this amazing truth, you will remain defeated in your life.

WHAT "MORE THAN ENOUGH" MEANS FOR YOU

There's a small chance you're even more jaded than I am. You listen to the verses in Habakkuk and read that God is more than enough, but you can't figure out how this truth should change your everyday life.

Let me help you out. Because God is enough, there is one thing you can be sure of:

Because God is enough, you can rejoice no matter what.

WE LIVE RIGHT beneath the surface of enough—always striving but never quite admitting that enough is, well, enough.

There's such incredible freedom in the truth that God is enough. Our joy isn't based on visible results in our life. God Himself is our reward. His salvation is our joy. There's always reason to sing.

No wonder Paul was able to say, "Rejoice in the Lord always; again I will say, rejoice" (Philippians 4:4). No wonder Peter said, "But rejoice insofar as you share Christ's sufferings, that you may also rejoice and be glad when his glory is revealed" (1 Peter 4:13).

You can sing when it's raining. You can take joy when your funds are low. Life is good in Christ Jesus, and it has nothing to do with what you're going through right now. The joy of the Lord is your strength.

Many Christians really struggle with maintaining joy while they're being stripped. I'd like to give you four ways that you can rejoice no matter your present circumstances.

1. Rejoice in who God is.

It doesn't matter whether your tree looks like it's blossoming or not. It doesn't matter if you see fruit on the vine. The reason you rejoice is the Lord. He is our reward. He is the only one who can fully satisfy the heart. He is our joy.

God's love is steadfast. He accepts us despite our failures. He is committed to us no matter what. He is no more impressed with our excellent performance as He is deterred by our failure. He is faithful God.

Even if nothing were to ever change in your life, you already have more than enough in Him. It's easy to become robotic about these truths:

♦ We have everything we need for life and godliness.
♦ We have been blessed with every spiritual blessing in the heavenly places.
♦ We have been chosen in Him before the foundation of the world.
♦ We have been predestined for adoption as sons.
♦ We have redemption, the forgiveness of sin.
♦ We have His love lavished upon us.
♦ We have a citizenship in heaven.
♦ We belong to the King.

May we never grow dull to the truths of the gospel. May we never lose the wonder of who God is.

2. Rejoice in what God has done.

Habakkuk rejoiced in his salvation when nothing else in his life looked very promising. Having grown up in the church, I can sometimes take my salvation for granted. I mean, doesn't everyone believe that Christ died for our sin to give us everlasting life?

I catch myself walking in and out of the doors of my church, flipping through the pages of my Bible, sometimes unmoved by the greatest story ever told: Jesus Christ, God's Son, humbly became a perfect man, bearing my sin and shame on the cross so that I could be free.

Nothing will deflate your heart like losing the wonder of what God has done for you on the cross.

3. Rejoice in what He is doing in you.

Do you still question what God is doing in your life? You may not see it right now, but His hand is mightily at work in you.

A kid recently came to see me with a large, twenty-centimeter laceration to his foot. The edges of the wound were ragged. I warned the boy that it would be painful at first. He clenched his mother's hand while I injected the stinging, numbing medicine. He teared up but didn't cry. He ground his teeth and waited. I took a pair of scissors and trimmed the dead edges of the wound. For a while, the cut looked bad, even worse than when I'd started. I wasn't satisfied until all of the ragged edges were made smooth. I then took my hemostats, hooked a needle on them, and got to work.

It wasn't easy. It took a long time to fix. But by the time I was done, the foot was made whole again. The scar will forever remain, reminding the young man of exactly where he's been.

When Christ called us to follow Him, we came to Him

with gaping lacerations and jarring defects in our lives. We should have been afraid of our wounds; instead, we hid in fear from Him—our gentle Healer. The moment we let go and trusted Him to fix us was the

WITH CHRIST at our lead, we're headed to higher places.

moment we realized that the pain wasn't as bad as we first thought. The longer He's worked on our wounds, the less pain we feel. He has even given us fair warning of the pain that is to come.

God's healing process can sometimes feel slow and tedious. It requires care and patience. But eventually the work is done, leaving us with a scar. When we finally look down, we notice that our feet look a little bit like hinds' feet, with scars reminding us of where we've been, and where we're headed. The hind's feet are exactly what we need, because with Christ at our lead, we're headed to higher places.

You may not see what God is up to right this moment, but His hand hasn't stopped working on you. Give it enough time, and you'll see: God is transforming you into His likeness and before you know it, you'll be ready to scale new heights.

4. Rejoice in what you can look forward to.

It's not over yet. Some of you are still at the beginning of your journey, others are halfway through, and still others are almost home. As long as you've got breath in your lungs, the journey home is not over.

Are you living with a sense of great expectation in your life? I'm not talking about more money or more fame or even more results for God's kingdom. I'm talking about looking forward to seeing Him someday.

Peter was as hardheaded as they come. He blew it at the cross and was stripped of every bit of pride and self-sufficiency. Through his failure was born a man utterly dependent on the Lord Jesus Christ and ready to receive all God had in store for him. Peter's heart was lit for Christ through his own stripping. The result was Pentecost where three thousand people received Christ as their Savior through Peter's preaching.

By the time you get to the end of his life, Peter has learned so much. But mostly, Peter has learned that nothing in this life compares to the hope of seeing Jesus someday. In 1 Peter 1:8 here's how he describes that anticipation: "Though you have not seen him, you love him. Though you do not now see him, you believe in him and rejoice with joy that is inexpressible and filled with glory."

Peter understood what it means to have true joy in the midst of some of the most difficult circumstances. He was a man transformed. He was now scaling the high places with hind's feet.

I'm learning too. I'm learning that the things of this earth pale in comparison to what's to come. I'm learning that no human goal is higher than the goal of knowing and loving Jesus my Lord. I'm learning to confidently say "yes" instead of "why me?" when the road gets bumpy and the mountains too steep.

God is more than enough. His Word is sufficient. His presence is all I need. God has proven Himself to be more than enough for me.

Do you know Him, this Jesus of Nazareth? Do you trust Him, this Savior of the world? Have you found Him to be more than enough?

> "Follow me, and I will make you fishers of men. Immediately they left their nets and followed him." (Matthew 4:19–20)

You heard Christ's call once and you answered yes. May your yes be stronger right now than it was on that day.

Appendix

WORLD CHANGERS

All heroes are shadows of Christ. —JOHN PIPER

I t will be worth it all.

In my pursuit of God and in following His call for my life I have often asked myself if it will be worth it all someday. I have often secretly questioned whether the sacrifice of knowing Jesus is worth the pain. At the height of my pain I have doubted God's ways, and almost given up.

My own sinfulness and humanness have revealed that in my weakness only God's grace sustains me and keeps me going. My story is a story of His grace. Since God's Word is life, it seems fitting to leave you with more of His words from Hebrews 6:9–12:

> Though we speak in this way, yet in your case, beloved, we feel sure of better things—things that belong to salvation. For God is not unjust so as to overlook your work and the love that you have shown for his name in serving the saints, as you still do. And we desire each one of you to show the same earnestness to have the full assurance of hope until the end, so that you may not be sluggish, but imitators of those who through faith and patience inherit the promises.

It will be worth it all someday. We will in time look back on these numbered days and wonder at their brevity. We will marvel at God's patience with us and reflect on His love. Until then, I have found that very little has encouraged my heart to go on more than the lives of the men and women who have walked the same paths we are walking today and have proven to be faithful to Christ's call to the end. They have completed their courses with joy and their stories remain a vivid example in history for those of us who long to make it safely home.

In these final pages, I will share with you some of the best stories of men and women who changed their world for Christ. They did it through the pain of being stripped. They did it by learning that only Jesus Christ can satisfy our deepest longings, and only His grace will keep us secure to the end.

Until we make it home, may we find in Him all we need and may we pursue Him passionately like our lives depend on it—because if you stop and think about it, they do depend on it.

GEORGE MATHESON (1842–1906)

Blind Scottish Preacher.

Wrote "O Love That Will Not Let Me Go."

"Matheson was blind, but with the eyes of his heart he
could see farther than most of us."
—Warren W. Wiersbe

Born in Glasgow, the eldest of eight children, George
Matheson had poor eyesight from birth. This did not
keep him from enrolling in the University of Glasgow at age
nineteen to study theology, with the hopes of becoming a
preacher.

It was during his time at the university that George completely lost his eyesight. It is reported that George had been
engaged to be married, but upon hearing that her fiancé was
going blind, the young lady broke off the engagement, telling
George, "Why, I couldn't be married to a blind man."

Nonetheless George would go on to a life in ministry,
pastoring a church in Innellan, Scotland. His sister cared for
him until the day she got married.

His sister's marriage was a difficult blow for George, as
he had become so dependent on her for his work. George
wrote the famous hymn "O Love That Will Not Let Me Go"
on the evening of her wedding. Here's what George had to

say about that night in a quote from his journal:

> My hymn was composed in the manse of Inellan on the evening of June 6, 1882. I was at that time alone. It was the day of my sister's marriage and the rest of my family were staying overnight in Glasgow. Something had happened to me which was known only to myself, and which caused me the most severe mental suffering. The hymn was the fruit of that suffering. It was the quickest bit of work I ever did in my life. I had the impression of having it dictated to me by some inward voice than of working it out myself. I am quite sure that the whole work was completed in five minutes, and equally sure that it never received at my hands any retouching or correction. I have no natural gift of rhythm. All the other verses I have written are manufactured articles; this came like a dayspring from on high. I have never been able to gain once more the same fervor in verse.[12]

Out of suffering comes much fruit. Out of loneliness comes great communion with Christ. George Matheson is an example of a life stripped for God's great glory. Today many of us continue to sing this hymn reminding us that we can have joy and peace in the midst of our sufferings.

> O Love that wilt not let me go,
> I rest my weary soul in thee;
> I give thee back the life I owe,
> That in thine ocean depths its flow
> May richer, fuller be.

O light that foll'west all my way,
I yield my flick'ring torch to thee;
My heart restores its borrowed ray,
That in thy sunshine's blaze its day
May brighter, fairer be.

O Joy that seekest me through pain,
I cannot close my heart to thee;
I trace the rainbow through the rain,
And feel the promise is not vain,
That morn shall tearless be.

O Cross that liftest up my head,
I dare not ask to fly from thee;
I lay in dust life's glory dead,
And from the ground there blossoms red
Life that shall endless be.[13]

ELISABETH ELLIOT (1926–)

Missionary to Ecuador.

Author and speaker.

"There is nothing worth living for,
unless it is worth dying for."

There is no better example of the stripped life than the life of Elisabeth Elliot. Born in Belgium to missionary parents, Elisabeth grew up in the U.S. and attended Wheaton College for her university studies.

It was at Wheaton College that Elisabeth met and fell in love with Jim Elliot. Theirs is a well-known love story, documented in detail in Elisabeth's book *Passion and Purity*. Though the couple was strongly and passionately in love, they went their separate ways with Jim feeling the Lord had called him to be a missionary to Ecuador and that he should stay unmarried. Their love story seemed to be cut short.

God had other plans for this couple though. Shortly after surrendering their love to the Lord, God in His grace brought Jim and Elisabeth back together. Life seemed brighter. Elisabeth was serving the Lord with the man she was deeply in love with. What could go wrong now?

One hopeful morning, Jim and four of his missionary friends headed to an unreached village of the Auca tribe. They had felt called by God to deliver the gospel to the Auca tribe. They had prayed for open doors to share the gospel. They had longed to see the Aucas come to know Jesus. They had confidence that God would work. Little did they know that that morning five missionary families would lose their husbands and fathers in what seemed like senseless murder by members of the Auca tribe. Jim and Elisabeth's daughter, Valerie, was just ten months old when Jim was killed.

One would think that a widowed mother and her ten-month-old baby would leave Ecuador and head back to the safety of home. But Elisabeth Elliot was never one to do the obvious. Utterly surrendered to the Lord Jesus Christ, Elisabeth stayed in Ecuador, bringing the gospel to the very people who had killed her husband on that hopeful morning.

Elisabeth remained in Ecuador until 1963. The Auca Indians gave Elisabeth the tribal name *Gikari*, Huao for "woodpecker," perhaps because she was willing to go where few had gone and to persist where few would have persisted. Many came to know the Lord through her surrender to God's call.

In 1969 Elisabeth married again, this time to Addison Leitch, a professor of theology at Gordon-Conwell Theological Seminary. It seemed as if life had settled down for Elisabeth, but her stripping process was not quite over. In 1973 Leitch died of cancer.

Elisabeth married a third time to Lars Gren, a hospital chaplain. Elisabeth is well known for her many writings that have influenced hundreds of thousands of young men and women everywhere, proving again that the life that God strips is the life He intends to use for His glory and honor.

HORATIO SPAFFORD (1828–1888)

꧁ ✦ ꧂

Chicago Lawyer.

Hymn writer famous for "It Is Well with My Soul."

I suppose life was smooth for Horatio Spafford and his family at first. They were well known in Chicago in the 1860s, and they loved the Lord. Horatio was a close friend of D. L. Moody, the famous Chicago preacher.

No one would have predicted the troubles that Horatio would suffer.

In 1870, Spafford's only son died of scarlet fever at the age of four. A year later came another great blow. Horatio had invested heavily in real estate on the shores of Lake Michigan. In 1870 the Great Chicago Fire wiped out every one of Horatio's holdings. The family was shaken. It seemed like a good time for Horatio to take his wife and four daughters on a holiday to England. Horatio thought it was providential timing, as D. L. Moody would be speaking on an evangelistic campaign in Britain at that time, and so Horatio made plans to join him in serving the Lord.

Though he had planned on traveling with his family, some unforeseen business held him up, and he was forced to delay. Anxious to get his family the rest they needed, he persuaded his wife, Anna, to go on ahead without him.

It was only nine days later that Horatio received a telegram from his wife in Wales. It read: *Saved alone.*

The ship Anna and the girls were on had collided with another English vessel, causing the greatest tragedy for the

Spaffords yet. The ship sank in twelve minutes, claiming 226 lives including Horatio's four girls.

Horatio quickly boarded the next ship out of New York to join his bereaved wife. It is told that during that voyage, the captain of the ship called Horatio to the bridge, pointing him to the site of the tragedy that had claimed his four daughters.

Horatio then returned to his cabin and penned the lyrics of one of the greatest hymns of all times: "It Is Well with My Soul."

It seems unfathomable to maintain unwavering faith in the face of such disasters, but Horatio Spafford understood a secret that few really grasp in this life—that life with Jesus Christ is safety, and that no matter the pain here on this earth, heaven is coming soon, and peace is in the person of Christ.

When peace, like a river, attendeth my way,
When sorrows like sea billows roll;
Whatever my lot, Thou has taught me to say,
It is well, it is well, with my soul.

It is well, with my soul,
It is well, it is well,
with my soul.

Though Satan should buffet, though trials should come,
Let this blest assurance control,
That Christ has regarded my helpless estate,

STRIPPED

And hath shed His own blood for my soul.
My sin, oh, the bliss of this glorious thought!
My sin, not in part but the whole,
Is nailed to the cross, and I bear it no more,
Praise the Lord, praise the Lord, O my soul!

And Lord, haste the day when my faith shall be sight,
The clouds be rolled back as a scroll;
The trump shall resound, and the Lord shall descend,
Even so, it is well with my soul.[14]

JOHN BUNYAN (1628–1688)

---◆---

Preacher.

Author of *The Pilgrim's Progress.*

J ohn Bunyan was born in England to a poor, working-class family. His father was a tinker, and John learned the same trade. Though he did not have much formal schooling, he did spend a brief time in boarding school where he learned to read and write.

One day, John Bunyan overheard several poor women conversing about the work of Christ in their hearts. He tried to join in the conversation but had no idea what they were saying. John wrote the following about that day:

> Their talk . . . was about a new birth, the work of God on their hearts, also how they were convinced of their miserable state by nature. They talked how God had visited their souls with His love in the Lord Jesus, and with what words and promises they had been refreshed, comforted, and supported against the temptations of the devil.[15]

It was a turning point for John. Those same women would introduce him to their pastor, John Gifford. It was under his preaching that John at last came to Christ. John would later preach at that same church where Gifford had pastored. He became known for boldly preaching God's Word anywhere he went.

The church at large was divided during that time.

The Anglican royalists attacked the nonconformist Baptist preachers and soon made it illegal to preach in non-approved places. In 1660 John Bunyan was arrested for preaching God's Word in a field near a farmhouse. He was asked to apologize to the magistrates and refrain from preaching, much like Peter and John in Acts 4. John refused. He was placed in prison for twelve years.

While most of us would consider prison an unjust result for preaching God's Word, John turned his prison into an extremely prolific time for writing. It was in prison that John wrote *Grace Abounding to the Chief of Sinners*, *Confessions of Faith*, and *A Defense of the Doctrine of Justification, by Faith in Jesus Christ*. John began writing *The Pilgrim's Progress* while in prison as well.

Little could John have predicted that this little book would become what is often said to be the greatest bestseller of all time, next to the Bible. By the time of Bunyan's death in 1688, eleven editions of *The Pilgrim's Progress* had been published with over 100,000 copies in print. Today this book has been translated into over two hundred languages and has changed countless lives—all from the stripped down walls of a prison cell. It is a reminder that though serving the Lord may result in the removal of earthly comforts from the lives of Christ's followers, nothing can ever touch the soul of the heart captured by the love of God.

FANNY CROSBY (1820–1915)

———◆———

Blind hymn writer.

Wrote "Blessed Assurance" and over 8,000 hymns.

"This is my story, this is my song,
praising my Savior, all the day long."

Fanny Crosby was born in New York in 1820 and became blind at six weeks of age because of a mistake by a physician during a period of illness. Despite her physical limitations, Fanny's life was a very productive one.

Fanny's father died while she was still young, and her mother sought domestic work to help support the family, leaving Fanny in the care of her grandmother Eunice. It was Eunice who set about to educate Fanny and helped her memorize great portions of the Bible. Fanny soon met the God of the Bible and when discouraged, she would turn to the Lord in prayer and ask for help, refusing to let her handicap limit her.

She wrote her very first poem as a child expressing her perspective so well:

> O what a happy soul am I!
> Although I cannot see,
> I am resolved that in this world,
> Contented I will be.
> How many blessings I enjoy,
> That other people don't.
> To weep and sigh because I'm blind,
> I cannot and I won't! [16]

At age fourteen, Fanny began attending a school for the blind that would become a haven. She would later teach in that school and meet many great men and women of that era including several presidents. She met Alexander Van Alystyne, a fellow instructor at the school, and married him at age thirty-eight. They had a baby who died shortly after birth.

Fanny Crosby wrote some of the greatest hymns of all time: "A Shelter in the Time of Storm," "All the Way My Savior Leads Me," "Blessed Assurance," "I Am Thine, O Lord," "Jesus Is Calling," "Praise Him, Praise Him," "Redeemed," "Safe in the Arms of Jesus," "Take the World but Give Me Jesus," and "To God Be the Glory," just to name a few.

Her life is an example of a woman who was undaunted by her physical limitations and who God used to change the world. While most of us would consider blindness a hindrance to doing great works for the Lord, Fanny always held to this belief:

Mother, if I had a choice, I would still choose to remain blind . . . for when I die, the first face I will ever see will be the face of my blessed Savior.[17]

JONI EARECKSON TADA (1949–)

Author, speaker, and artist.

Founder of Joni and Friends.

Joni grew up in an idyllic Christian home. She was the youngest of four girls and greatly enjoyed sports and the outdoors. In 1967 after her graduation from high school, Joni went swimming with some friends in Chesapeake Bay. On that fateful day she dove into the water and broke her neck. She became a quadriplegic.

The next few months were extremely difficult for Joni as she struggled with depression and despair. Before the accident she had felt that she wasn't living the life she should be, so she had prayed that God would change her. After months of staring at the ceiling and wallowing in her depression, Joni began to wonder if this was indeed God's answer to her prayer.

Under the influence of friends and with the prayers of many, Joni surrendered her disability to the Lord and began immersing herself in God's Word.

Little did Joni know what lay ahead for her in the years to come. Joni has been a influential author of our time, with nearly fifty books to her credit. She is an artist and speaker and founder of Joni and Friends, an organization that advocates for the handicapped. Her name is well known throughout the world as a lover of Jesus Christ. She has a daily radio ministry reaching millions of people with the good news of the gospel.

She is known to have signed all of her paintings with "Joni Eareckson, PTL" (Praise the Lord). Joni also loves to sing praise songs and has several recordings of her music.

In 1982 she married Ken Tada and they still live in Southern California today. As if being quadriplegic is not challenging enough, Joni was recently diagnosed with breast cancer, though it's said that she has a hopeful prognosis.

Joni's testimony is particularly personal to me. I was ten years old when I saw the movie *Joni* in Beirut, Lebanon. It was the first time I recall having a deep longing to follow the same God that Joni worships. It was the first time I understood that God can take a broken life and heal it for His glory. My life hasn't been the same since.

That God would allow harm to His children seems preposterous, yet Joni's life is a vivid example of how God uses our pain and suffering for His glory. He triumphs over your difficult circumstances and shows Himself mighty in the life that trustfully surrenders to His will.

HUDSON TAYLOR (1832–1905)

———— ✦ ————

Founder of China Inland Mission.

"He must move men through God—by prayer."
—philosophy of Hudson Taylor

No man has exemplified greater faith through prayer than the man Hudson Taylor. His very salvation was a result of the prayers of his mother. At seventeen, Hudson went to his father's library in search of a book. He came across a gospel tract and picked it up thinking to read the story at the beginning of it. At that same moment, his mother felt a strong leading to pray for her son. "Thus," said Hudson, "while my dear mother was praising God on her knees in her chamber, I was praising Him in the old warehouse to which I had gone alone to read at my leisure this little book."[18]

It wasn't long after his salvation that Hudson felt God's call to China. It was a powerful and personal call that would change the course of his life and grow him into one of the greatest men of faith in our modern history.

In preparation for life in China, Hudson Taylor moved to one of the poorest areas in England to study medicine. It was during these years that Taylor began testing God with His promises. In giving, he sacrificed his last dime trusting the Lord to provide for his need. He would pray that his forgetful boss would remember to pay him, rather than ask for his salary when the time for payment had passed. To Hudson Taylor, it was simple: If he couldn't trust the Lord to meet his needs in England, how could he expect Him to provide for him in China?

By the time Hudson set sail for China, his prayers were expectant and his faith mature. He would need strong faith as the work in China would not be easy. Apart from the challenges of being a missionary in a foreign land, Hudson Taylor lost his wife and several of his children while in China. He himself suffered physical ailments that at one point forced his return to England. But Hudson Taylor was undeterred. Having been called to China, Hudson would endure to the end.

Hudson Taylor staked everything on the words of Jesus: "Whatsoever ye shall ask in my name, that will I do" (John 14:13 KJV). He believed, as Jesus taught, that the heavenly Father is not embarrassed by any shortage of supplies and that, if we ask in childlike trust, our every need will be supplied. "Depend on it," he contended, "God's work, done in God's way, will never lack God's supplies."[19]

Hudson Taylor spent fifty-one years in China and founded the China Inland Mission in 1865. The CIM remains in existence today and continues to touch souls for God's kingdom.

JOHN AND BETTY STAM
JOHN: 1907–1934, BETTY: 1906–1934

————— ✦ —————

Missionaries to China.

Martyred for their faith.

They had given up everything to move to China with their three-month-old daughter with one goal in mind: to share the good news of Jesus Christ with the lost.

On the morning of their arrest, John and Betty were warned that the communists were headed to their small village. It didn't seem to be too big a threat at first, but within hours, it became evident that John and Betty's safety was in danger.

By the end of that day, John and Betty were arrested by the communists and taken into custody with their daughter. That night John wrote a letter to his missionary organization asking for help, but the letter was never delivered. The letter was later found bundled in Betty's clothes. In it John paraphrased from Philippians 1:20, "May Christ be glorified, whether by life or death." His words would be prophetic.

The morning after their arrest, the couple was forced to walk twelve miles to the next location. When the group stopped for the night, Betty hid her daughter, Helen, inside a sleeping bag. The next morning, John and Betty were taken to their deaths. Many lined the streets to watch. One Chinese shopkeeper tried to persuade the communists not to kill the Stams. When he wouldn't step back despite the soldiers' orders, the man's home was invaded. In his house, a

Chinese copy of the Holy Bible and a hymnbook were found. He too would be killed with the Stams that day for his faith.

After marching for a bit longer, John was ordered to kneel, and he was beheaded while Betty watched. Betty and the shopkeeper were killed moments later.

Baby Helen was found two days later by a Chinese pastor. She was taken by him and cared for. She was then safely delivered to her grandparents, also missionaries in China.

Though Satan's goal was to destroy the work of Christ, the martyrdom of John and Betty Stam would inspire many to become missionaries for the gospel. One may wonder where God was on the day of John and Betty's arrest. One may wonder why God didn't deliver them from their violent deaths. But John and Betty Stam understood that life here on earth was temporary and that eternity is forever.

Stripped here on earth, but forever reigning with Christ in glory.

May the name of the Lord Jesus Christ be forever praised both now and in eternity.

World Changers

MY STORY

Notes

1. Os Guinness, *The Call: Finding and Fulfilling the Central Purpose of Your Life* (Nashville: Thomas Nelson, 2003), 4.

2. John Bunyan, *The Pilgrim's Progress in Modern English*, revised and updated by L. Edward Hazelbaker (Alachua, FL: Bridge-Logos, 1998), 4–5.

3. David Livingstone quoted in J. E. Chambliss, *The Life and Labors of David Livingstone, LL.D, D.L.C.* (Philadelphia: Hubbard Bros, 1875), 313–14. Ebook.

4. Joseph M. Scriven, "What a Friend We Have in Jesus," *NetHymnal*, January 18, 2013. www.cyberhymnal.org/htm/o/l/oltwnlmg.htm.

5. Oswald Chambers, "The Place of Exaltation," *My Utmost for His Highest*, October 1, 2012. utmost.org/the-place-of-exaltation/.

6. Oswald Chambers, "God's Silence—Then What?" *My Utmost for His Highest*, October 11, 2012. utmost.org/god's-silence—-then-what/.

7. Helen H. Lemmel, "Turn Your Eyes upon Jesus," *NetHymnal*, January 18, 2013. www.cyberhymnal.org/htm/+/u/turnyour.htm.

8. P. C. M. quoted in L. B. E. Cowman, *Streams in the Desert* (Grand Rapids, MI: Zondervan, 2008), 250.

9. Unknown author quoted in Cowman, *Streams*, 314–15.

10. Max Lucado, *When God Whispers Your Name* (Nashville: Thomas Nelson, 1999), 32–33.

11. *Random House Webster's College Dictionary*, Revised & Updated (New York: Random House, 2005).

12. Donald Macmillan, *The Life of George Matheson, D.D., LL.D, F.R.S.E* (New York: A.C. Armstrong and Son, 1908), 181.

13. George Matheson, "O Love That Will Not Let Me Go," *NetHymnal*, January 18, 2013. http://www.cyberhymnal.org/htm/o/l/oltwnlmg.htm.

14. Horatio G. Spafford, "It Is Well With My Soul," *NetHymnal*, January 18, 2013. http://www.cyberhymnal.org/htm/i/t/i/itiswell.htm.

15. John Bunyan, *Grace Abounding to the Chief of Sinners* (Oxford: Ginn & Company, 1910), 17. Ebook.

16. Fanny Crosby quoted in Anne Adams, "Fanny Crosby, Hymnwriter," *History's Women*, 2005. http://www.historyswomen.com/women offaith/abigail2.htm.

17. Fanny Crosby quoted in Gene Fedele, *Heroes of the Faith* (Alachua, FL: Bridge Logos Foundation, 2003), 209. Ebook.

18. Hudson Taylor quoted in Howard and Geraldine Taylor, *Hudson Taylor in Early Years* (New York: Hodder & Stoughton, 1912), 68. Ebook.

19. Hudson Taylor quoted in Howard and Geraldine Taylor, *Hudson Taylor's Spiritual Secret* (Chicago: Moody Publishers, 2009), 121.

Acknowledgments

Second books are harder to write than first ones. The author now has expectations to measure up to but hasn't written enough to know what's normal yet. Yet one thing is obvious: the list of people who make any project happen only grows with time.

I'd like to start by thanking my friend and publisher, Holly Kisly, whose input and support I value more than I can express. The entire Moody Publishers team and René Hanebutt have made my life as an author as smooth and successful as I could have dreamed.

I am so thankful for Rob Eager who has done his share to help me find my voice. I appreciate him more than he could tell on any given day.

I want to profusely thank the readers of my blog. They are my fellow companions on this journey home. They love me daily by showing up each morning. They press me onward and upward, and I love them. Shirley is my favorite reader and has become my friend. She prays for me daily, and I am forever grateful.

I continue to be deeply thankful for my editor, Bailey Utecht. There's nothing I love more than giving away my manuscript to her as an indication that it is finished!

Thanks to my church family at Harvest Bible Chapel, particularly the women I shepherd. You have allowed me to lead you well and have been used by God to grow me. Thank you.

I love my pastor, James MacDonald, and his wife. They

continue to be a steady source of love and support to me.

Thank you to my dear friends Lynne Tellschow, Renee Gilman, and Tina Watschke. You have held my arms up, and words cannot express my gratitude for you.

To Bonnie Brztowski I owe a part of my brain. She remains the most faithful and hardest-working assistant that anyone can have, but she is also my dear friend.

Lisa Harper is a genius and I am so thankful for her. She has supported me from day one. Lisa also introduced me to some amazing women of the faith. I'm grateful especially for Sheila Walsh, Lisa Bevere, and Christine Caine. They are women who love God and love people. I am a better Christian because of their example and appreciate how they have poured into me and continue to do so.

Lastly but most importantly, I'd like to thank my family. None of this would be remotely possible without the certitude that you are 100 percent behind me in heart and soul. You have loved me unconditionally and walked with me every stripped step of the way. You remain a light and a source of grace when I feel unloved and uncertain. Special mention goes to Diana who always feels the brunt of my pain, my mom who has functioned like a step-in for the Holy Spirit, and my father who remains the wisest man I know. Thank you for loving daily.

My heart is more deeply in love with Jesus Christ today than it has ever been. None of this would be possible without Him. I've said it before and I'll say it again: May the Lord Jesus Christ be magnified through me always or shut me up forever.